Off the Map

Around the Salcombe–Kingsbridge and Dart Estuaries

3rd edition

Jane Fitzgerald

with Trudy Turrell

Photographs by Kate Mount

GREEN  BOOKS

with South Devon AONB

This edition published in July 2005
by Green Books Ltd
Foxhole, Dartington
Totnes, Devon TQ9 6EB

in association with South Hams District Council

Previous editions published in 2000 and 2002
in association with South Hams District Council

Printed by Latimer Trend & Company, Plymouth, UK
on Fineblade Extra paper, made from low-chlorine pulp

British Library Cataloguing in Publication Data
available on request

ISBN 1 903998 56 5

Contents

Acknowledgements

So many people have contributed to the making of this new edition that it is impossible to name all of them; however, I would particularly like to thank Kate Mount, Nicola Kennedy, Peter and Matt Burner, Malcolm Barnett, Tony Hoile, and Victoria and James Hannaford. My thanks also go out to Trudy Turrell and the team at the South Hams AONB for their support, and in particular to John Elford and all at Green Books for making it happen.

Foreword to the Third Edition

Off the Map started with a series of lists left on the kitchen table: lists for friends who'd come to stay and wanted a few tips as to where to go and what to do. As they didn't care much for driving in the lanes, everything listed had to be reached by foot, ferry or bike. Over time, these lists became itineraries. These in turn became the bones of the book.

We are into a third, even bigger edition. Lots of changes have taken place since 2002, particularly in the burgeoning area of local produce—this needs a book to itself to keep up with the changes. New to this edition are four beginners' guides, in which local enthusiasts outline how to get started with surfing, fishing, diving and sailing. Their tips, I hope, will take some of the slog out of starting from scratch.

Off the Map is not a prescriptive guide: rather, it is my aim that readers will create their own itineraries around the material in the book, and in so doing stumble across surprising discoveries of their own. If this is the case, we'd love to hear of these new finds—please send details to us c/o the publishers, Green Books.

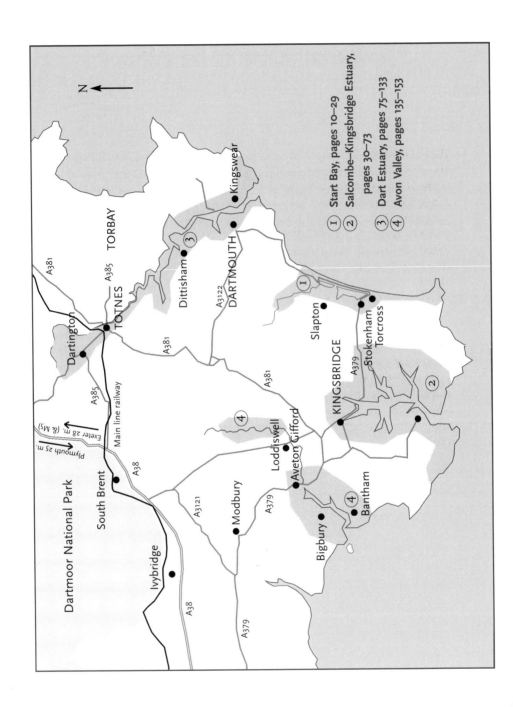

N

Dartmoor National Park

South Brent

Ivybridge

A38

Modbury

A3121

A379

Bigbury

Bantham

④

Aveton
Gifford

Loddiswell

④

A379

Plymouth 25 m.

Exeter 28 m. (& M5)

Main line railway

A385

A38

Dartington

A385

TOTNES

A381

A381

A381

KINGSBRIDGE

A379

Stokenham

Torcross

②

Slapton

①

DARTMOUTH

A3122

Dittisham

③

TORBAY

A381

Kingswear

① Start Bay, pages 10–29

② Salcombe–Kingsbridge Estuary,
   pages 30–73

③ Dart Estuary, pages 75–133

④ Avon Valley, pages 135–153

A Different Kind of Travel Book

Tucked between the slopes of southern Dartmoor and the sea, the South Hams is a land of river valleys. Five rivers define the landscape, threading through the hills and offering many a 'sheltered place'—which is the Anglo-Saxon meaning of 'ham'.

Before the advent of the modern road system, transport was much easier by water than through the high-banked twisting packhorse tracks. Each valley was quite remote and inaccessible, and so developed its own character. It is just these particularities of place that *Off the Map* tries to identify.

Although many of the remotest spots can now be reached by car, *Off the Map* encourages the reader to go at a slower pace. We suggest you visit one or two valleys in detail, and soak up the atmosphere through encounters with the people, by tasting local foods and enjoying the process of travelling itself, whether on foot, by bus, bicycle or boat. *Off the Map* is not all inclusive: it reflects one person's likes and interests. Superb places, businesses and activities have inevitably been omitted, and others will have changed hands by the time you read this book. I hope *Off the Map* will prove useful to dip into, and that it may initiate many eventful journeys of one sort or another.

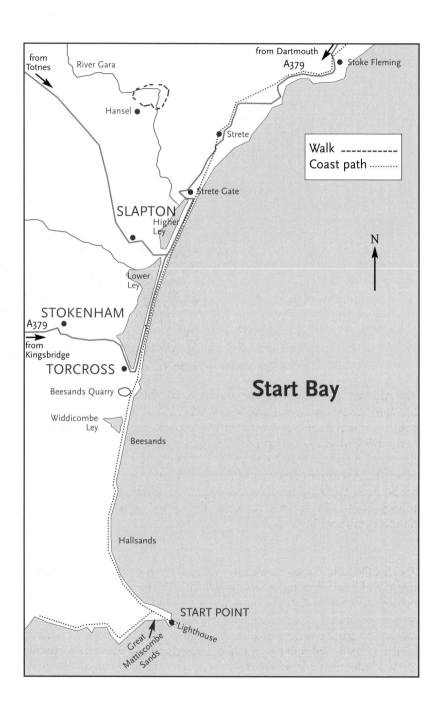

from
Totnes

River Gara

from Dartmouth

A379

Stoke Fleming

Hansel

Strete

Walk ----------
Coast path ··········

Strete Gate

SLAPTON

Higher
Ley

N

Lower
Ley

STOKENHAM

A379

from
Kingsbridge

TORCROSS

Beesands Quarry

Start Bay

Widdicombe
Ley

Beesands

Hallsands

START POINT

Lighthouse

Great
Mattiscombe
Sands

Chapter 1: Start Bay

This chapter covers the 4 km long 'line' or shingle
ridge between Strete Gate and Torcross. Detours are
taken inland to the villages of Slapton and Stokenham,
before continuing along the coastal path to
Beesands, Hallsands and Start Point.

The urge to race cars along the leyside road which runs the length of
Slapton Sands has something to do with the revelation of flat open
country, which forms such a contrast to a landscape veined with sunken
lanes, tall hedgerows and whaleback hills. This sudden encounter with
the very flat and the very long can trigger desires to run, fly, or otherwise
cover the distance as fast as possible—which is not recommended. *Off
the Map*, on the other hand, would suggest travelling by bus. For one of
the joys of Start Bay is that it can be easily reached from both Kingsbridge
and Salcombe, with buses running every hour.

Strete Gate

This is called after the gate which prevented cattle grazing along the shingle
ridge, and from straying up to the village of Strete. There was once an
estuary near Strete Gate, but now the River Gara is reduced to a small
stream which runs through silted marshland. The Manor House Hotel and
its tropical garden once stood on the sheltered site beside the car park,
which is now dotted with sturdy tables, cleared grassy areas and a barbecue.
Bring a butterfly guide, as all kinds can be spotted feeding on the buddleia.

On a raised mound is a viewing point which indicates landmarks to be seen across the bay: Slapton Line and Leys are clearly visible, as are the village of Torcross and the lighthouse at the end of Start Point.

Following the River Gara upstream from Strete Gate into the Gara Valley is impossible by foot, as the fields are very marshy. It is possible, however, to discover this remote and thickly wooded valley from the road which descends via the hamlet of Hansel.

The Gara Valley

The River Gara rises in high ground near Halwell, about six miles from its mouth. Its course runs though some of the most beautiful parts of the South Hams, through countryside mostly unchanged by this century. Around Hansel, a mile or two upstream from Strete Gate, the valley sides are so steep as to be almost impassable. Along its short course, which once powered five mills, are small stone bridges.

Gara Valley Walk

Land around the Gara is privately owned, but there is a wonderful walk to be had either by entering the valley on the Slapton side and following the lane down past Merrifield, or alternatively along past Fuge, off the Strete road. Walking in from the Slapton direction, follow the lane down for about one mile into the valley. After the sharp bend just past Hansel, a lane bears off to the right: this leads down to Lower North Mill and a small bridge which crosses the Gara. On the bank by the bridge, the ancient stone remains of some mill workers' cottages are visible. For those who lived here a century or more ago, everyday life here was both remote and hard, despite the beauty of the countryside.

After the bridge the path bears round to the left and leads back up the valley to 'Snail's Castle'—a house reputedly built for a Victorian mistress—perched on the cliffs overlooking the Gara. The cartoonist and impressionist painter Jack Yeats (see opposite) lived there at the turn of the century; his more famous brother, the poet and writer W.B.Yeats, and John Masefield were both regular visitors. John Masefield's book *Jim Davis* (an adventure story for boys) is set in the valley.

The lane continues past Snail's Castle to Orestone—a house where the horses were changed after their long haul with flour from the mills below—and eventually leads to the Fuge road at the top of the valley. The gateway here opens on to a panoramic view of the valley, widening towards the coast. Alternatively, to end up on the Slapton side of the

WRITERS AND ARTISTS OF THE GARA VALLEY

Valerie Belsey, author of *Discovering Green Lanes* and *Exploring Green Lanes in the South Hams,* talks about some of the secrets held by the green lanes of the Gara Valley.

In the National Gallery of Dublin in May 1999, a gallery was opened, dedicated to Ireland's most famous painter, Jack B. Yeats. Amongst the sketches, water colours and oils, is an old sepia photograph taken at the turn of the century which shows Jack and his wife Cottie standing in front of their home 'Cashlauna Shelmiddy'—Snail's Castle in the Gara Valley.

Jack Yeats was born in Ireland, the son of a barrister turned portrait painter. At the turn of the century Jack married a Devon girl, moved down to Strete, and lived here for 13 years. Until then he had been making a name for himself working on black-and-white magazine illustrations for, amongst others, *Paddock Life* and *The Vegetarian.* His sketches showed great humour, something which was to be continued in his sketchbooks which deal with life in and around the Gara Valley. Yeats built a studio, now in ruins below the house, and spent his days sketching the valley, the sunken lanes, local fairs, circuses, races, shows and gypsies.

During his time in the valley he collected ballads and poems, which he published firstly through the Cuala Press, one of the most famous being John Masefield's 'Cargoes'. Masefield visited 'Snail's Castle' and wrote part of his novel *Jim Davis* there. Together they spent a lot of time constructing and racing toy boats along the Gara, both of them always dressed meticulously in suits and straw hats.

Although Yeats seemed to have lived a fairly reclusive life in the valley, there was one group of Strete residents who came into full contact with the great man—the children who attended the Strete National School (the building is now 'The Laughing Monk' restaurant). Jack and his wife were passionate about the theatre productions which were shown at the National School for the children at Christmas time. They had such thrilling titles as: 'Timothy Coombewest', 'The Wonderful Travellers' and 'The Gamesome Princes and the Pursuing Policemen'. The writers and artists of the Gara Valley had a lot to celebrate.

valley, take the lane down below Orestone that leads to Higher North Mill (this might be the time to pick up some freshly laid eggs). Wild flowers are in abundance: orchids, highly perfumed white violets, and daffodils in spring. The turning back down to Lower North Mill is five minutes walk back towards Hansel from Higher North Mill.

A word of warning: some of the walking is rocky and steep; the rest is along quiet lanes. As there is nowhere to leave cars in the valley, parking in Strete would be recommended.

Slapton Sands

'Sands' is a bit of a misnomer, for I doubt whether the shingle will enjoy sand status for a good few thousand years. On the other hand, this shingle does shimmer—and is golden, thanks to eroded flint fragments which somehow shifted to Slapton from the sea bed twenty-five miles away—and it doesn't get in your sandwiches. Mixed with the flint are granite fragments brought down from Dartmoor by the River Dart; also

schists, slates and quartzite. At the north end of the beach, the rising cliffs provide some shelter. Along here stood the small village of Strete Undercliffe, destroyed by the great gale in 1708. In the cliff face, some joist holes and the remains of a wall are all that are left of the village.

Even on warm days, Strete Gate is rarely crowded. The steeply shelving beach provides good swimming, and the water is clear and blue. In the late afternoon, with the sun declining to the west, there is a peculiarly clear, warm Devon light. Locals come down here to unwind after a day's work.

Slapton Ley

'The Barre of sand betwixt sea and lande'—as sixteenth century topographer John Leyland described Slapton Line—is a strangely mobile landform, as the storm of 11th January 2001 testifies. The road has now

Pictures of the Lower Ley

been repaired, but managing transport routes at the edge of a constantly moving coastline is a challenge. It's a delicate balance between nature, communities and the forces of global warming and shifting sands. Observing Slapton Line as a giant nature laboratory, the nearby Field Centre are noticing signs of recolonisation of the extraordinary collection of salt-tolerant plants which blaze along the shingle ridge in early summer.

Slapton Ley is a National Nature Reserve. The Ley is a freshwater lake—the largest in south-west England—and is separated from the sea only by the narrow shingle bar, or 'line' as it is known locally. Slapton Ley is really two Leys, a higher and a lower. The Lower Ley, an open freshwater lake with a thick reed fringe, is a well known pike fishery; and the Higher Ley is a lake now silted up with marsh and vegetation. The surrounding marshes and reedbeds provide excellent feeding and breeding grounds for all sorts of wildlife. Over four hundred and ninety species of plants have been recorded, including the nationally rare strapwort. Slapton is also particularly well known for its diversity of birdlife: ornithologists come to catch

NATURE'S FLOTSAM

Anywhere between Torcross and Start Point you can expect the unexpected. Along the tideline are washed up all kinds of curiosities—the natural ones, not man-made plastics and tar. Look on the strands of seaweed and see the grey crustings growing on their fronds. These are sea-mats and sea-firs, colonial animals rather than plants; fascinating under a magnifying glass. Empty sea shells are there—oval trough shells and whelk shells, usually orange-pink and looking like giant, spired snail shells. If you see a ball of papery bubbles, these will be the egg cases laid in the sea by the whelks. White, oval discs, up to about 9 inches (20 cms) long, are the chalky skeletons of cuttlefish. The brown or black pouches, with tendrils or spikes sticking out from the four corners, are the cases where baby dogfish or rays developed. The brown ones with tendrils were laid by dogfish, and the black ones with spikes were laid by a species of skate or ray. The commonest are the purses of thornback rays. All of them are popularly known as 'mermaids' purses'.

sight of rare migrants and other birds which stop off on their long and arduous flights. A sighting of the Great White Egret was recorded in 1994.

Thatching Reed has been grown at the Ley for centuries. It was cut and stacked in the autumn, for use in thatch, incorporated in cob buildings and for screens and garden fences. Before the construction of the road in 1856, the existing track was made more passable with reeds from the freshwater side of the line and with crushed shells and shingle from the beach. Each year, five acres of reeds are still cut by hand sickle and put into stooks in the traditional way.

Huntin', shootin' and fishin' In the eighteenth and nineteenth centuries, the Ley was used for shooting, and there was an annual coot shoot in February to which most of the village turned out. In the 1920s and 1930s Slapton was a popular resort with wildfowlers and pike fishermen. The Royal Sands Hotel stood on the seaward side of the shingle ridge. An ivy-clad building with stone mullioned windows, the Royal Sands luxuriously accommodated shooting and fishing parties. Men and

A SEASIDE GARDEN

Early summer evenings are the time to see the wild flowers at Slapton. Amongst the seashore garden which blazes along the top of Strete Gate beach look out for sea radish; a bushy plant, nearly waist high. In summer it produces masses of small, pale yellow flowers. In autumn greenfinches come to feast on the seeds in the swollen pods—and in summer so can we, for when the pods are small and tender they taste just like garden radishes. Nationally it is a rare plant, but here along the south-west coast it is abundant. So are the sea carrot, sea mayweed, restharrow and sea campion. It's also possible to wander through a forest of viper's bugloss flower spikes—around two feet tall with masses of blue, bugle-shaped flowers up the stem. Its usual habitat is chalk downland. What's it doing at Strete? The answer is in the soil—or rather the shells in the shingle. The calcium from the millions of wave-broken seashells provides the nutrition needed by viper's bugloss and several other plants which thrive here.

boys from Slapton village acted as ghillies, accompanying the guests and showing them the whereabouts of pike. In return they were given a beer at lunchtime and half-a-crown for the day's work. Pike—'of patriarchal age and size'—were displayed in glass cases in The Royal Sands. When Slapton was evacuated in 1943, the hotel had already fallen into ruin. It was finally demolished when 'Pincher' Luscombe, a collie from Slapton, triggered six land mines as he scrambled under barbed wire.

The Field Studies Council at Slapton Ley Field Centre manages the two hundred hectare National Nature Reserve which includes both Leys, the Line, deciduous woods and fast-flowing feeder streams. Herbert Whitely (the founder of Paignton Zoo) owned a large estate, of which the Nature Reserve was just a part. On his death in 1960, the estate was broken up, and the unproductive land—the Reserve—was leased to the Field Studies Council on the proviso that it be used for the dual purposes of conservation and education. **Slapton Ley Field Centre** thus came into being: it is a thriving centre of excellence, and runs courses which cater for a multitude of interests, throughout the year.

Staff at the Centre recommend autumn as a good time to visit, both for the quietness of the place and for the extraordinary collection of visiting birds. To see the starlings roosting at the Ley is an eerie experience, with echoes of Dante (his image of the souls of the damned in the Inferno)—loud, gigantic clouds of them in their tens of thousands. Autumn is also the time for fungi, of which over 2000 species have been recorded in and around the Ley.

For the Passing Visitor The Centre is a very friendly place. A welcoming reception area provides information on walks, fishing, recent bird sightings and forthcoming events. In the summer holidays, the Field Centre runs a week-long summer safari which is five full days of activities such as scavenging in rock pools, mini-beast hunting, shelter building and sculptures on the sands. You can book for the whole week or a single day should you wish, and there is a regular programme of guided walks. Call in at the Centre for a leaflet. Opportunities for walking around the reserve are plentiful. The route around the Ley is especially recommended for those with young children, as it offers plenty of distractions along the way, such as contained Leyside beaches, boardwalks, bridges, and wildlife to be appreciated at any level—from insects to swans to rabbits, and all free of charge. For fishing enthusiasts, clinker-built rowing boats may be hired on the Lower Ley for perch, rudd, roach and the occasional pike. **Fishing licences** may be obtained at the Field Centre. **Slapton Ley Field Centre** ☎ 01548 580466.

Slapton Village

In *A Fortunate Place*, his excellent book on Slapton, Robin Stanes writes:

> Even as late as 1830 a resident remarked how remote Slapton was, how
> unsophisticated its people, and maybe it is this isolation that has produced
> the individual character and 'culture' of the area, the local breeds of cattle
> and sheep, dialect words, place names, and so on.

It is no wonder that a drawbridge once protected Slapton village from
wandering Bretons. For, from the point of view of an early settler, Slapton
was a very good bet. In a site sheltered from the wind, with fertile soil and
abundant supplies of water, as well as stone, wood and reed, and with
fish also in constant supply, the conditions were enviable. It is said that
most South Hams villages were self-sufficient in all but salt and iron. For
Slapton, iron was all that was missing. A remote place, some nine miles
from the nearest markets, difficult to reach by road, Slapton grew
through the centuries to be a fiercely independent community.

Not all, though, were as independent (or wilful) as Lady Judith
Hawkins, the lady of the manor at Pool who, when she walked to church
at Slapton in the mid 1600s, made it her business to walk the whole
distance along a red carpet, laid before her by two black servants to stop
her shoes from getting muddy. She was 'remembered longest and best
by the people of Slapton'.

With its narrow streets, earthy colours and tightly packed houses,
Slapton explodes with flowers in springtime. Its sheltered position, soft
climate and fertile soil allows for some splendid gardens and very early
flowering. The waxen blooms of the early magnolias in Vale House and
the secret garden of the Chantry are welcome beacons of spring. As I
write, there are two gardens in Slapton which open on occasion to the
public: Tor Wood, and Meadow Court.

The Chantry This terracotta-
coloured building above the
church, from which is slung the
high footbridge over the road, is a
later addition to the original
collegiate chantry founded by
local aristocrat Sir Guy de Brian
in 1373, with the provision that
on May 31 (St Petronilla's day) a
funeral mass be sung for his

> **SEA KALE**
>
> Slapton was noted for its sea kale, long
> known in the south-west as a table
> vegetable, but not introduced into
> gardens until the mid 1700s. A certain
> Mr Southcote of Stoke Fleming was the
> first to cultivate it for kitchen use in his
> garden in 1775.

SLAPTON COMMUNITY WEBSITE

'Save Slapton Coast Road' is a sticker seen on back windscreens in Slapton, where the community is striving to keep the A379 coastal road to Strete, Stoke Fleming and Dartmouth open. It was damaged by ferocious weather in 2001, and since then the future of the road has hung in the balance.

It was the strength of feeling about the road that combined with powerful community spirit to create Slapton Community website, **www.slapton.org**. The site is packed with up-to-date news, information about village events, associations and residents and a historical archive. As well as a gallery showing work of local artists, it gives details of local businesses, and lists holiday accommodation around the village. There is a short story, games pages and 'Adam's page' which records local resident Adam's endeavours (with the help of his Dad) to create a web page.

soul. The Chantry was the last of its kind to be built in England before their suppression in 1545. All that now remains of it is the ruined tower, which can be seen from the garden of **The Tower Inn.** At dusk on a summer's evening, it is the perfect place to ponder the ancient stones of the tower and watch the resident bats dart in and out of the crumbling walls. **The Tower Inn ☎ 01548 580216.**

Below the Chantry is Slapton Church, dedicated to St James. Built of local Charleton stone in the fourteenth and fifteenth centuries, it is unusual for its spire, one of only three in the whole of the South Hams. Some of the seventeenth-century village cottages are still thatched, though the reed from the Ley is no longer in use. House repairs in the village have revealed the reed to have been in common use in the construction of cob walls. Shell fragments from the shingle are still apparent in the older renders, and the local stone is much in evidence in walls, coping stones and paving.

There are around thirty holiday cottages in the village, and during the tourist season the number of incomers equals, if not exceeds, the locals. But the village still thrives, with its own community composting scheme and an excellent local shop—a visit to which is a must. It keeps local cauliflowers from Loworthy Farm in season, and other vegetables from local growers. Honey from the village is also stocked. For local events, look for notices on the bus shelter or in the shop. The horticultural show in August is also not to be missed.

Start Bay Centre Housed in the old school building just outside

Slapton, the Start Bay Centre is an educational field centre used by schools and other organisations. At certain times of year it may be hired privately by large parties. ☎ 01548 580321.

Camp Site The camping and caravanning club site is noted as a fine site with very good facilities. It also has the advantage that both the beach and the Ley are a stone's throw away. A great base for exploring the area. **Camping and Caravanning Club Slapton Site, Middle Grounds, Slapton ☎ 01548 580538. www.campingandcaravanningclub.co.uk.**

Horse riding at Dittiscombe Alex Farleigh runs a thriving riding stables at Dittiscombe, just beyond the hamlet of Pittaford outside Slapton. There are both indoor and outdoor schools. Lessons or hacks may be arranged at all levels. Riding is an enormously popular activity in south Devon, with events nearly every weekend. **Dittiscombe Equestrian Centre ☎ 01548 581049.**

Torcross

Bang on the sea, the village of Torcross gets the worst of the weather. The sea front houses line up stoically, scoured by salt spray, barely protected by the stout sea wall which rears up from the beach. In contrast to its sheltered inland neighbour Slapton, Torcross stands exposed at the south end of the Leyside drag. Until the 1600s it was probably no more than a cluster of fishermen's cellars, as before that time the threat of pirate raids made it impossible to live beside the sea. A fishing community then established itself and stayed. In his account in 1920, James Fairweather describes the scene as the women of Torcross pulled in the nets:

. . . from ruddy bright lasses to old dames of seventy years and upwards, whose bleached hair escapes from the great flapping sun bonnets which cover their heads They all wear painted canvas skirts, and stand holding a rope. . . . A few minutes and the boat is up with a veritable boil in the water, occasioned by the frantic gambols of the fish. The men pull a semicircle round the school and quickly land on the other side.

Although one or two boats still work from Torcross, the fishing community has all but disappeared. Today, lone anglers dot themselves along the beach, huddled over their lines.

Fish of the 'and chips' variety are immensely popular at the **Start Bay**

Torcross, beyond the water

SUNDAY LUNCH SHOPPING
AROUND STOKENHAM—THE FUN WAY

First gather your vegetables at **Stokeley Barton Farm** shop, about a half mile walk up the road from Torcross towards Stokenham. A visit here can take as long as you want, for ' pick your own' is an option. Children love the activity of gathering their own food, and take great pride in their pickings. Strawberries in June are the favourite. It's a bit of a trek to some of the fields, but worth every step for the view alone, as they stand high above the bay. Red, earthy potatoes in a number of varieties are available at the shop, and for those with large car boots, a sack or two make great presents to take back home. A detour to the plant area, where the collection of perennials and shrubs gets better and better, is recommended. **Stokeley Barton Farm Shop, Stokenham. ☎ 01548 581010.** Opening times: Winter 9.30–5.30. Summer 9.30–6.30.

Set apart from the other shops at Torcross is **Hannaford's** the butchers. This family-run butcher's shop was part of the family farm. The shop has been in existence for 103 years and sells the best of local meat and game. There's no messing with pre-packaging here: the carcass is hauled down from its hook and the meat is cut in front of the customer. It's a friendly family business, known to give the occasional sweet to children on Saturdays (but that's a

secret). Orders may be placed by phone. Hannaford's van calls at some villages. Ring for details. **Hannaford's, Torcross ☎ 01548 580209.**

Finally, cool off with a swim, throw stones at a stone tower, and bury as many feet as possible.

Richard Hannaford, Torcross

Inn at Torcross. The family who run this pub have made it their business to do justice to traditional English fish and chips. The fish is locally caught and fantastically fresh, the chips chunky and crisp. The trimmings are unpretentious, and sauces come in sachets. If you've come for a more sophisticated meal, watch out for the specials on the blackboard— the skate wings and black butter is

simple and delicious; so are the scallops. The family room fills up rapidly, and can be rather raucous, so get there early, for they don't take bookings. **The Start Bay Inn, Torcross ☎ 01548 580553.**

Stokenham

A mile or so inland from Torcross is Stokenham, a pretty village with a thriving church, school and two pubs. Stokenham has a flourishing garden society, whose plant sales are immensely popular. The flower festival in August makes a terrific show, with the traditional leeks, chrysanths, gladdies and spuds. The church also puts on a flower festival which involves fruit, flowers, seeds and vegetables being put together in quite unexpected ways. Another high point in Stokenham is the local **Craft Fair** at the end of July.

Just about every aspect of the architecture of a village church tells a story. Most are open to visitors (if not, ask in the local shop or pub whether it can be opened up for a visit). The **Church of St Michael and All Angels** in Stokenham is no exception. Records of 1198 refer to a church in Stokenham dedicated to St

> ### SPRING GREENS
>
> If you take a walk to Beesands in the spring, why not pick your own salad or greens to complement the freshest of fish? Try a mixture of young dandelion, corn salad, winter-cress, sorrel and young hawthorn and beech leaves—or try sea beet, a good substitute for spinach.
>
> Sea beet grows in giant glossy clumps beside almost every seashore, estuary and river. Pick the youngest fleshy leaves—they smell and taste like spinach so it's easy to identify. Cook as spinach—there's no need to add salt as the leaves have their own salty taste. Lovely in a croissant, split and warmed with a little feta cheese.

View from Stokeley Barton Farm

Humbert. This changed to St Barnabas in 1786, and latterly to the Church of St Michael and All Angels. Some details to note:

The Belfry The lofty west tower and peal of six bells has local blue slate louvres in the belfry, in which the apertures are unusually wide to allow the peals to sound out over what is still a very scattered parish. **South Porch** Cut into the stone work of the left hand door jamb is a rough cross, possibly a votive cross made by someone in the middle ages to remind them of a vow taken. **Holy Well** This was used to feed the church pond (where the car park now is). It is situated on the left hand side, above Church House. Its water was noted as a cure for eye disease. **The Sanctuary** A chair to the left of the altar belonged to a Reverend Henry Sherwood (b. Truro 1781), who had the distinction of being the first missionary to Persia, and translated the Bible into Persian. **Green Men** Built into the south wall is an early fourteenth-century double *piscina*, discovered during repairs in 1846. The brackets of the arches are carved with heads issuing branches from their mouths. **South Transept** The window shows the wreck of the 'Spirit of the Ocean', which was stranded on the rocks off Start Point on March 23rd 1888. Twenty-eight sailors drowned; they are buried in a mass grave near the lych gate at the top of the churchyard.

Torcross to Beesands

To walk southwards from Torcross to Beesands, take the Chapel steps on the seaward side of the Torcross Apartment Hotel. The route is marked with the coastal path acorn sign. The first bit is quite a climb, but at the top there's a fine view along the sweep of 'The Line' back to Strete Gate.

Beesands Quarry

Before reaching Beesand Cellars, there is an opening which leads into a disused slate quarry, which at the time of writing is unsafe to enter. Once inside this vast steep-sided enclosure, the sands of the sea disappear and quiet descends, interrupted only by the odd riff of birdsong or rustle in the undergrowth. A path leads along the quarry basin beside the remains of a pond which was once stocked with colossal goldfish.

Beesands

This seaside village has undergone quite a transformation in recent years. The village green which runs behind the beach used to be dominated by a vast caravan park, packed with an army of green vans. Following their removal, Beesands has picked itself up and become a very desirable place to live. Nevertheless, it has utterly resisted being prettified, and held on to the look and feel of a working village.

The Bird Hide Past the houses at the north end of Beesands village, at the back of the green, is a small car park: there is a gate, and a short pathway which leads to Widdicombe Ley. Built on to the marsh is a bird hide, allowing intimate views of life on and around the marsh. The hide's existence is kept pretty quiet, and a visit to it feels like a privilege.

Shellfish Fishing was the main-stay of this small isolated community for centuries.

Although this is no longer the case, the Hutchings family, who have been fishing from Beesands for generations, still run their fishing business from here. Fred Hutchings, a Beesander (known locally as Zanderlins) is the last remaining fisherman working all year round from his beach boats. **Britannia Shellfish Ltd** supplies crabs, lobsters, crevettes and a host of other shellfish to some of the top kitchens in the country. For the likes of you or me, wanting the odd crab or a kilo of mussels, Britannia Shellfish open up their tanks in the afternoon. How much fresher can you get? For the lily-livered, the Hutchings will dress lobster or crab for you, but for this they need notice. Wet fish is also on sale when available. Opening times vary—ring to check. **Britannia Shellfish, The Viviers, Beesands. Office ☎ 01548 581186, Tanks ☎ 01548 581168.**

The Cricket Inn If ever a warm place was needed for refuge, it's on a cold day at Beesands. The Cricket Inn, on the front at

Angler fish at Beesands

Beesands, provides just this, with fine ales on tap and an extensive menu to revive the flagging visitor. **The Cricket Inn, Beesands ☎ 01548 580215.**

The Chapel The door to this tiny Edwardian chapel is usually open, and it has a very intimate feeling. On a wall inside is a memorial to villagers killed in 1942. Built almost on the beach, on a blustery day the strains of the elderly harmonium must be muffled by the breakers.

Hallsands

The ruined village of Hallsands, which was washed away in 1917, is visible from the coast path, where there is a viewing platform and a board telling the story of Hallsands with archive photographs. It is no longer possible to walk amongst this mix of the domestic with the elemental as the path down to Hallsands beach has also been washed away. 'The hamlet of Hallsands itself looks as if it properly belonged to the sea, and only been borrowed from it for a time.' James Fairweather, writing in his 1912 guide to the area, made an uncanny prediction of the village's fate.

Crowded on to this rock ledge were thirty-seven cottages plus a pub, shop and post office. The whole village was just forty feet wide. Almost all Hallsands' 128 residents were involved in fishing. Not only did the women haul the boats in, but they also carried their menfolk to the boats on their backs so that they didn't start the day with wet feet.

Although the village had no harbour, a wide shingle ridge used to exist in front of this rocky ledge and this protected the houses from the sea. It was when the banks of shingle just offshore were dredged to make concrete for Plymouth's dockyards, that the shape of Hallsands beach began to change. The sea did not naturally replace the shingle, as the dredging company had promised, and after 650,000 tonnes of shingle were removed, the beach dropped by 20 feet, bringing the sea right up to the sea walls which protected the village.

After being battered by storms in 1903 and 1904, a combination of high tides and strong winds on 26th January 1917 brought the sea

Fred and Jean Hutchings bringing up the catch

WIDDICOMBE LEY

The Devon Birdwatching and Preservation Society has built a hide behind the lake at Widdicombe Ley. A path goes from the car park, round the back of the Ley to the hide. From it you have a grandstand view of mallard and coot, Canada geese and the resident swans. A pair of great crested grebes usually nest there. You are surrounded by the rasping, chattering song of reed warblers and may see one, a small, brown-backed bird perched on a swaying reed.

As well as mallard there are other duck. The diving duck are mostly tufted duck; the males are black and white, and their mates are brown. Slightly larger and less common are the pochard. The drake pochard are grey-backed with a reddish head and the females duck-brown again. Of the dabbling duck, the black-tailed gadwall and the chestnut-sided, shovel-billed shoveller are regular at Beesands. In midsummer, drakes of many species of duck lose their bright plumage and resemble their dowdy partners—this is called 'eclipse plumage'. By autumn the brown tips to the feathers are wearing off and the bright colours are beginning to reappear. In mid-September you may see the first wigeon, and some of the drakes will be just emerging from eclipse plumage and have beautiful pink and ginger tints. They are duck which nest mostly in eastern Europe and spend the winter with us. Not only do the drakes have striking colours, they also make an eerie sound—a shrill whistle which brings back memories of winter days on the estuaries and marshes of Devon.

crashing into the village. All the cottages bar one were completely destroyed and the villagers left homeless. And now there is only one cottage and a few walls left standing, this remote fishing village is visited by students from all round the world—an object lesson in the effects of man tampering with environmental systems he doesn't fully understand.

Hard by the coast path is **Trout's Apartments**, named after the first owners of the building: Ella, Patience and Edith Trout. Much has been written about the Trout sisters, who built the original hotel on the proceeds secured through Ella, in 1917, having bravely rescued a sailor in difficulty. The sisters laid the foundations themselves, stone by stone. These leathery and legendary women caught their own fish and grew all the vegetables for their guests. After the deaths of Patience and Ella, Edith struggled to run the hotel on her own. It closed in 1959, but she remained there as a recluse for seventeen years—with the tables all set for dinner—until her death in 1978. From Easter through till October, al fresco meals and snacks are available at Trout's Servery between 11 and 6, and if the weather's unkind there are a few tables to sit at in the warmth of the conservatory. **Trout's Servery, South Hallsands ☎ 01548 511174.**

SEADOGS

Newfoundland dogs were as essential to the fishermen in the villages around Start as the sheepdog is to the farmer. When the sea was too rough for boats to come close enough to throw a rope, it was the dog's part to fling itself into the waves and, thoroughly buffeted by the swell, swim close enough to the boat to grab hold of the rope between its teeth and swim back to shore.

KITTIWAKES

A new sound has been added to the waves and the wind at Hallsands. A few years ago the colony of kittiwakes moved from Start Point to the cliffs below Trouts, which echo with the birds' cries: 'Kitti-wake, kitti-wake, kitti-wake!' The colony has grown to several hundred pairs. Kittiwakes are proper seagulls, spending the winter out in the Atlantic, far from shore. In March and April they return to prospect for their nesting sites. In April you can watch the pairs building their nests on the vertical cliffs. They mould mud, muck and seaweed to cement a cup-shaped nest to the narrow ledges. The beaks are pale yellow, but the gape inside, when they open their beaks, is bright orange. Dozens of them sit on the ledges in pairs, nodding their heads and caressing each other's necks. When they fly off over the sea, you can see that the wing tips are completely black with no white specks. The legs also are black.

START POINT LIGHTHOUSE

Start Point Lighthouse is situated on the headland of one of the most exposed peninsulas on the English coast, cutting into the sea for almost a mile. The tall circular white tower with battlemented parapet was designed in the Gothic style by James Walker in 1836, and has been guiding vessels in passage along the English Channel and past the dangers of the Skerries Bank for over 150 years. Its characteristic signal of three flashes every ten seconds, powered by a 1 kilowatt MBI lamp, focused by a third-order catadioptric based on an 1844 design by Alan Stevenson (uncle of the author of *Dr. Jekyll and Mr. Hyde*), reaches an intensity of 200,000 candela and can be seen for 25 miles out to sea.

These rather abstract technical facts and figures become much more impressive as the visitor climbs up the final and steepest flight of stairs to the top of the lighthouse and wonders at the dedication and resilience of the men who kept the light burning in all weathers for the 123 years before it was electrified in 1959. The lighthouse was automated in 1993 and is now controlled via a telemetry link from the Trinity House Operations Control Centre at Harwich.

Open to the public since 1999, the curious visitor is introduced to the workings of this extraordinary building by a well informed guide. Whilst the maps marking the many wrecks in Start Bay and on the Skerries Bank point to the familiar role of the lighthouse as a hazard warning, the set of faded flags that were formerly used to communicate with all ships entering the Channel, and send manual signals about their cargo, destination and levies due via the chain of coastguard houses as far up the coast as Southampton, are an intriguing insight into a far less familiar maritime communications system. On a clear day, though, it's the view around the Point from 62 metres above mean high water that makes the climb worth every step. Open at half terms and from Easter to end September. Contact Kingsbridge Tourist Information Centre for opening times.

Start Point

Blackstone Rock lies off Start Point, as does the Skerries Bank—a shingle bank deposited by the shoreline currents. The two combine to make Start Point a notoriously hard stretch to navigate in bad weather: the sea bed is scattered with the wreckage of vessels which never made it. Walking around Start Point needs care, for at places on the western side of the peninsula the steep rocky sides simply fall away into an often ferocious sea.

The made-up road from the car park to the lighthouse is altogether tamer, and the going far easier. Whichever route you take, the blast of sea air, combined with the sheer power of the land and seascape, is very bracing.

Mattiscombe Beach At Start Point car park, beside the gate and stile leading in the direction of the lighthouse, is a path to the right. This leads down to Mattiscombe Beach. The walk down is about 15 minutes, and again it's important to watch children closely once through the gate at the seaward end of the path. Consult the tide table before a visit; low tide allows for more exploration, less fretful rock climbing, and space to play. It's a good beach for swimming, and some tame surfing. The walk down there filters out many less adventurous beachgoers, and I've never known it truly crowded.

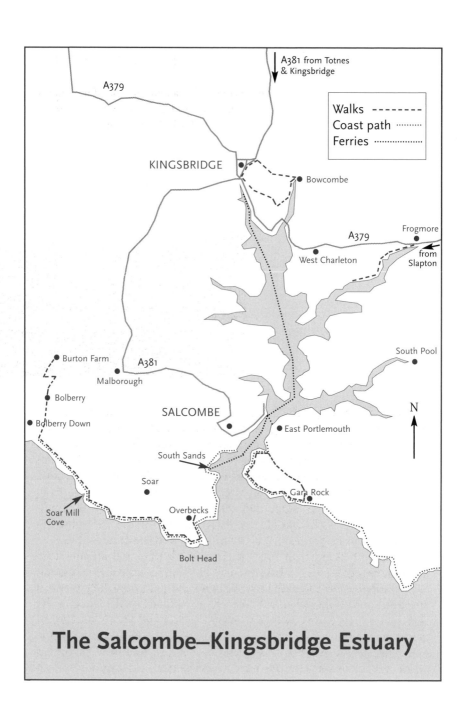

The Salcombe–Kingsbridge Estuary

Chapter 2: Salcombe–Kingsbridge Estuary

This chapter takes a journey around the estuary
from Salcombe to Kingsbridge, via the creeks of
South Pool, Frogmore and Bowcombe.

Salcombe

History Salcombe has the air of an island: entering the town, with its
jangling yachts and spiky vegetation, feels a little like going abroad. And
it is just this separateness and comparative inaccessibility which makes
Salcombe the distinctive place it is. By road, the journey is six miles from
Kingsbridge, and to East Portlemouth on the opposite bank many more.
Traditionally, the way to transport goods and people back and forth to
Salcombe has been by water, and with good reason—the route is infi-
nitely more practical, enjoyable, and far shorter. Readers are urged to
consider journeying at least one way by water, and the other by bus.

Exotic fruit Wine, fruit, cider, grain, wool, leather and timber—over
the centuries these waters have seen all kinds of goods come in and out
of the harbour. For Salcombe was a significant port, especially between
the 1860s and 1890s, when oak from the woodlands on the banks of the
estuary was transported by tugs to Evans, Bonker and Vivien, builders of
the fast and elegant Salcombe fruit schooners. These skimmed across the
seas at terrific speed to the Azores and West Indies, manned by minimal
crews who were seriously deprived of sleep (the less weight the boat

View of Salcombe

carried, the faster it sailed and the fresher the fruit when it reached English shores). By the 1890s Salcombe was falling over itself with new houses and villas built by wealthy sea captains, and almost everyone in the town was involved in some way with the industry. There were shipwrights, carpenters, shipsmiths, riggers and sailmakers, as well as all kinds of ancillary professions: builders, schoolteachers, even dressmakers who sewed fine dresses for the sea captains' wives, using bolts of silk and cottons brought home from overseas.

Decline set in when the competition from the northern shipyards became too fierce. It was at this time that the emphasis switched from shipbuilding, fishing and shipping, to tourism.

Salcombe Haven The Marine Hotel was the first hotel in Salcombe. When opened in 1880, visitors were registered weekly in the local paper. The steamboat from Kingsbridge to Salcombe was the first pleasure boat to bring visitors to the haven—before then, Salcombe was only accessible to those with their own transport. At the beginning of this century the steep northern side of the South Sands valley, which had belonged to the Earl of Devonshire, was sold off in plots. Gradually, more 'pleasure boxes' were built 'in a cautious fashion'. Salcombe in 1929 was described in a guidebook as 'a pleasant retreat with a little harbour alive with scudding sails of tiny craft, and popular with delicate patients who appreciate bathing and beautiful surroundings'.

Lotus eating After the second world war, Salcombe attracted ex-officers with gratuities to spend. Some took up shellfishing, while others bought luxury yachts for charter, cafés, pubs and restaurants.

The fishing that remains today is shell fishing: nine boats still operate from the fishing quay. The catch is mainly crab, spider crabs in particular. These are shipped off to France, where they are eaten as a delicacy. Otherwise it's mainly recreational fishing: out to sea for mackerel, or along the estuary for flounder, ray, trout and bass.

Sea Tractor at South Sands

Onshore at Salcombe

Exploring the town Approaching Salcombe by road, there is a steep pitch down into town. Glimpses of what's in store can be caught between the trees: sparkling blue water, fingers of distant creeks—and so many boats. As the harbour gets closer, so do the houses, muscling in on precious views of the sea and estuary—it is an extraordinary setting. The natural harbour around which the town has developed lies at the entrance to the sheltered Salcombe–Kingsbridge Estuary, on both sides of which are stretches of wild coastline.

The illusion of being on board is strong in this seaside haven, for even the rock on which the town is built is sea-green. Houses here borrow liberally from boats, assuming girls' names, with weather-boarding, flagpoles, lookout points and lifebelts gushing petunias.

One way to get a sense of the place is to explore the 'back doubles': a network of steps and paths cut into the steep rock, by which it is possible to traverse the entire town. It's a great way to keep fit, and an opportunity to catch those visceral views of backyards, gardens and workshops. For a breather, why not visit the **Holy Trinity Church** on Church Hill, where the tapestry kneelers have been painstakingly sewn by parishioners. Flowers, local scenes, association emblems, and naturally a lot of fish, boats and water: a parish map for knees.

Try to make time to visit the **Salcombe Maritime Museum** at the Council Hall in Market Street, below the Tourist Information Centre. This small museum run by local volunteers is stuffed with ephemera and information on Salcombe maritime history. There is a lot to see, so give yourself plenty of time, but beware of the French-style lunch hours. Bring your magnifying glass, as there's so much detail to soak in, stories to read, knots to learn and models to wonder at. **Salcombe Maritime Museum Council Hall Market Street ☎ 01548 843080.** Open Easter until the end of September, 10 am–12 and 2–4 pm.

THE SALCOMBE ALOE

In the garden of Cliff House in 1774, the first American Aloe (a stately exotic) on record bloomed. The flower stem which shot out from the 28 year old plant grew at a rate of 9 inches a day, until at the end of September it reached 28 ft, bearing innumerable flowers on 42 branches. Its leaves were 9 ft long and 6 inches wide.

The library, council offices and Salcombe Yacht Club are all based at **Cliff House**, a splendid Victorian building. The gardens below offer a lovely public space for reading the papers, having a picnic or simply watching the boats on the estuary.

Beside the Water

Beaches There's a ferry to South Sands from Whitestrand, and Mill Bay is accessible from the East Portlemouth Ferry (see Appendix). As its name might suggest, the sands at both North and South Sands are good for making castles. There is also safe swimming. Further seaward there is a cove with a small lagoon, good for spotting fish and edible crabs. Crabbing at Victoria Quay is a popular sport, and it's easy to get fixed up with a line and bait from the local fishing shops.

Sitting On a fine day, the Ferry Inn garden is ideal for watching the world float by. So too the Wardroom Café in Fore Street, and Cliff House Gardens.

Swimming in the Rain Maintain the illusion that it's warm and sunny beside the estuary, even if it's teeming down outside. **The Marine Hotel Waves Leisure Centre** is gloriously situated beside the water. There's a good sized pool, an exercise room, jacuzzi and sauna. Full-day tickets cost £10 for adults and £5 for a child (free for under fives, and weekly family tickets are available for £55. For those having Sunday lunch at the Marine, the leisure facilities are free of charge. **Marine Hotel, Cliff Road, Salcombe ☎ 01548 844444.**

Sheltered by high walls, this 20m heated outdoor pool in Onslow Road is for both serious swimmers

---

CRABBING

You will need: a crab line, purchased from any fishing shop; bait (bacon); a plastic bucket; and a high tide.

Sit on the edge of the harbour wall. Dangle bait into water pull them up and put them in the bucket. The person with the most crabs wins.

Tip them out and watch them all run back in the water amidst screams of delight from small children.

and sunbathers. Recently updated, it now has the luxury of warm changing rooms. The pool is filled from the end of April until late September. Times of opening are posted on the noticeboard outside, and it may be hired for private parties. Contact **Mrs J. Furness ☎ 01548 843799 or Mr P. Tobin ☎ 01548 844187** for details.

Crabbing at Victoria Quay

Salcombe

When shopping in Salcombe, be sure to bring a cool bag, for just below Shadycombe car park is the **Salcombe Dairy Ice Cream Factory Shop**, which stocks 'bin ends' of the local (and exceptionally good) ice cream. It might be a case of rum and raisin with only a smattering of raisins, or just an end of line; whatever the irregularity, it will be written on the box. Look out for cornets for children—masses of flavours to choose from. **Salcombe Dairy, Shadycombe Road** ☎ 01548 843228.

Island Street, below Salcombe Dairy, is the centre for boat maintenance, building and equipment. There are chandlers with new and second-hand gear, tantalising noticeboards with an assortment of boats for sale and craft for hire. Further along Island Street is **Yeoward and Dowie**, the place to pick up freshly caught crab and lobster. Thrill the children with a scary peek into the seawater tank in the warehouse!

Coves Quay Art Gallery. There's a huge amount of work to see at this compact first floor gallery. Owner Mandy de Haan has assembled a discerning collection of paintings, sculptures and ceramics from established and emerging artists in the South-west. Pieces are largely figurative, and many represent elements of the life, land and seascapes of Devon and Cornwall. I suggest a visit to see for yourself, there is such a range of work, and prices too—you can pick up a print for under £40. Mandy and staff are both welcoming and helpful, and there is a useful website which details forthcoming exhibitions and opening times. The Gallery is in the square opposite the Copper Shop in Thorning Street (a turning beside the jewellers in Island Street). **Coves Quay Art Gallery, 6 Coves Quay, Thorning Street** ☎ 01548 842666. **www.covesquay.co.uk.**

Making your way towards Fore Street you pass **Victoria Quay**, a hot spot for crabbing at high tide. Lines and bait are on sale at the boat hire kiosk opposite. The fishermen's cottages on your right are amongst the oldest buildings in Salcombe. Now much prettied up, they'd set you back a yacht or two.

Under the bridge at the Fortescue, you'll see a set of steps leading up to the **Loft Studio**. Salcombe has a thriving community of amateur artists, and this is their base. It's always worth a look at the exhibition. The quality of the work is mixed, but sometimes there are paintings of such exuberance, humour or sharp observation that you're strongly tempted to buy one—at a very fair price, too.

Dinghy racing at Salcombe

Salcombe

Go over the road from the loft and turn left: a little way down is **The Oil Seller**, which stocks a profusion of things to make you feel good. **The Oil Seller, 10 Clifton Place ☎ 01548 843003.**

Back on to Fore Street (the main shopping street in Salcombe): there's a lot of space given over to marine clothing. Sights are set on the 'yachties', and collections are certainly up-market, but you pay for the clothes to be hardwearing, practical and high performing. So if you want to invest in a Musto, Helly Hansen, or a pair of Soliado deck shoes, where better to do so?

For a present with a difference, why not choose one which has been across the world and back? Jon Alsop, a local sail-maker, had the bright idea of recycling used sails in the form of hardy bags and jackets. The range can be seen at the Sail Loft. **Jon Alsop Sailmaker, Croft Road ☎ 01548 843702.**

Up past Lloyds Bank is **The Tree House**, a toyshop that's a bit out of the ordinary. It holds a diverting stock of toys, puzzles, games and tricks, assembled by a man who seems to have a direct line to what children want, not what granny and grandpa think they want.

The Treehouse, 61b Fore Street ☎ 01548 844133. Generally, food is expensive in Salcombe. There are no large supermarkets, except for a Spar shop at the top of town. At the bottom of town, **Cranch's Pantry** is a good friendly general food store. To pacify small people and give comfort to some big ones, **Cranch's Sweet Shop** still sells sweets in jars: penny chews, fried eggs, gobstoppers, sherbert dips, and for chocolate-lovers, Cocoa Tree chocolates hand-made in Chillington, with fondant fillings made from elderflowers from the hedgerows, blackcurrants from Stokeleigh and Dittisham plums. **The Upper Crust** bakery sells home-baked bread and wholesome pasties—a good place to stock up for a picnic. There is also a traditional butcher, and a fish shop where you can be sure of quality and freshness. **Cranch's Pantry & Fudge Shop, 78-80 Fore Street ☎ 01548 842331. The Upper Crust, 3 Fore Street ☎ 01548 842824.**

Salter's Bookshelf
The perfect place for holiday reading, for besides having a good selection of new paperbacks, Salter's has a book exchange. Lots of popular titles are to be bought for a fraction of the price of a new copy, and if the book is returned in good condition within two months of purchase you will be credited half the price to spend on another book. Salter's also keep philatelic accessories, and those little packets of exotic and extaordinarily shaped stamps which I hadn't seen for years. **Salter's Bookshelf 1 Russel Court ☎ 01548 844464.**

Eating Out

Eating out in Salcombe is patchy, and prices are on the high side. An all-day breakfast can set you back the price of a small dinghy. I suggest opting instead for the places with the coveted views; there isn't a huge difference in price. The **Wardroom Café, for example,** overlooks the ferry departure point. Here one can linger over coffee and home-made cake, while watching the comings and goings on the water. **The Wardroom, The Waterfront ☎ 01548 842620.**

The **Victoria Inn** is used by locals, and recommended for an inexpensive lunch. **Victoria Inn, Fore Street ☎ 01548 842604.**

For a rather special meal, **Catch 55** has a great atmosphere and a super

38

range of fish dishes.
At **Restaurant 42,**
blanquettes, blackboards,
symphonies, medleys,
chips and optics are just
some of the things you
won't find, for owners
Neil and Jane Storkey
determined to avoid all
the above when opening
their restaurant in Fore
Street in 2004. Between
them they have
transformed what was the
underbelly of the
Salcombe Hotel into a
bright yet mellow space of
honeys, creams, canvas,
wood and wicker. Slap
bang on the estuary, one
wall is almost entirely
glass, and beyond this is a
sunny terrace looking
across the water to
Millbay. Most tables are
round (so everyone can
talk to everyone else)
cutlery is weighty, and
linen white and crisp. As
for the food, fair to say the
chef (who arrived via the
Horn of Plenty), is wired
into the best of local
produce, buying fish
straight off the boats and
making full use of foods
foraged from the wild
such as wild garlic and

samphire. The
atmosphere is convivial
and relaxed, and the
prices are much softened
by the two for £42.00
offer which runs in all but
the height of the season.
Restaurant 42, Fore Street
☎ **01548 843408**
www.restaurant42.co.uk
Salcombe Coffee
Company is a child
friendly café serving tasty
fresh food at very fair
prices. At lunchtime there
is a choice of two home-
made soup and daily
specials as well as paninis
and filled baguettes.
Opens from 5.00—9.00
pm in the evening during
the season when any of
the grown up dishes can

be ordered as half
portions for the children
(who are kept occupied
with colouring sheets and
baskets full of toys). Even
pets are considered
here—outside, there is
always a bowl of water
and supply of biscuits for
the dog.
Children also enjoy a
trip to **Captain Flint's,**
which does a great home-
made pizza—fun food in
theatrical surroundings.
Catch 55, 55a Fore Street
☎ **01548 842646.**
Salcombe Coffee Company
73 Fore Street ☎ **01548**
842319 Captain Flint's
Restaurant, 82 Fore Street
☎ **01548 842357.**

Terrace of the Wardroom Café

Out from Salcombe

Salcombe has three ferries in operation in the summer months; here are some options for exploring the area using a mix of bus, ferry and leg power. The first is a coastal walk from Soar Mill Cove via Overbecks and South Sands to Salcombe itself. The second is a walk from Soar Mill Cove to Burton Farm at Galmpton. Finally there's a ferry trip to East Portlemouth and a walk along shaded leafy tracks to Gara Rock, returning by a spectacular stretch of coast path.

1. Soar Mill Cove to Salcombe Town Centre

(via Bolt Head, Sharpitor and South Sands: a four-mile coast path walk.) This walk covers a spectacular stretch of National Trust coastline. From Soar Mill Cove, follow the track to the coast path towards Bolt Head. Owned by the National Trust, this section of the coast path makes for comparatively easy walking, without the heart-stopping drops found on other parts of the route. Along the way, rugged rocky outcrops rise from short sheep-cropped grass. In late spring, spires of foxgloves line up amongst the gorse, and on warm days the air is thick with butterflies. Watch out for grey seals on the rocks below.

The stark promontory of Bolt Head offers splendid views towards Prawle Point, a good place to pause before descending into the valley behind Starehole Bay, where the shadow of the wreck of the Herzogin Cecile, lost in 1936, darkens the water; nearby a waterfall dives into the natural pool beside Bellhouse Rock. Moving up out of the

CAMPSITE AT BOLBERRY

A couple of miles outside of Salcombe in the hamlet of Bolberry is an excellent family-run campsite at Bolberry House Farm. There is loads of space. It's completely child friendly, very safe and the same families return there year after year (including local families!). There are sound washing and shower facilities (in the softest of spring water), a play area with table tennis, and children can bring their bikes. Pitches are very generous, and some have super views out to sea. A small site shop opens each morning in the high season, and there's a fish and chip van twice a week. There is a bus stop at the entrance to the park, taking away the hassle of beach car parking. **Bolberry House Farm, Bolberry, Malborough ☎ 01548 561251.**

GHOST STORY

After a particularly busy day at Overbecks, Alan Scott Davis, the then curator, was locking up and doing his rounds of the rooms, checking that all was in order. From the gallery above he heard noises. He was convinced that the house was empty, yet the noises grew louder. They weren't footsteps—more one footstep, then a dragging sound. Scott Davis then realised that in his later years Otto Overbeck had suffered a bad leg which was permanently bandaged, and the sound was that of him making his own nightly tour of the house.

valley, the path joins Courteney Way. The previous owners, the Courteney family, cut this path in the 1860s for their many shooting parties to make use of. They broke the tops off the vast rock pinnacles on the cliff top for walling—the local hornblende rock is comparatively soft, easily eroded by the salt-laden winds. Colours of the stone are grey or green, the green being more pronounced when the stone is wet. You'll notice it used in some of the old cottage walls around town. This is a fine place for bird-watching: peregrines nest in the cliff face, and gannets drop out of the sky, fishing for sand eels. It is home too for the little owl.

Nearing Sharpitor, the path becomes shaded by sweet chestnut and sycamore, and leads to the entrance of the National Trust property Overbecks.

Overbecks

When Otto Overbeck invented his electrical rejuvenator he believed it could tone and cure 'all illness with the exception of malformation and germ diseases'. He claimed the machine had 'practically renewed my youth. My age is 64 years, but I feel more like a man of thirty and I am mentally more alert'. When his quest for immortality of the body didn't succeed, Otto settled for being remembered as the man to catch the largest recorded carp, and on his death in 1937 he left his house and gardens to the National Trust on the condition that it should be named Overbecks after himself. Fifty years on, signposts still read Sharpitor, and that name remains in local currency. Sorry, Otto!

Overbecks House

The House Occupying a spectacular site, the house now contains Otto Overbeck's intriguing collection, with local additions. There is a maritime room, with artifacts, stories and pictures piecing together some of Salcombe's rich maritime history. In the Overbeck room is the rejuvenator, and a collection of 19th century dolls with disturbingly adult dress and features. The shells on show in this room were probably the mementoes of sailors, as are the examples of scrimshaw—the decorated ostrich egg and sperm whale tooth. Hidden under the stairs there is a secret room especially for children. It is full of dolls and toys, including exquisitely detailed dolls house settings. A 15–minute ride on the rocking horse was a reward for the best pupil of the week in Salcombe School.

A further proviso in Otto Overbeck's bequest was that there should be a youth hostel as part of the estate, and so there is. Occupying a position that four-star hotels would die for, part of the main house is given over to the YHA. What better place to wake up in the morning!

The Gardens Christopher Lloyd, the garden writer, refers to Overbecks' gardens as having a 'too good to be true setting'. Terraced into the hillside 60 metres above the estuary, and sheltered by woodlands and cliffs, the gardens enjoy a remarkably mild microclimate. Tender plants thrive and

The gardens at Overbecks

AND THEY RUBBED IT
WITH CAMPHORATED
OIL . . .

Pick up a dropped leaf from a camphor tree in the gardens of Overbecks. Crush it and smell it. Wood from the camphor tree has a particular smell, a little similar to eucalyptus. The wood was used in China for making clothes chests—the perfume from the wood kept the clothes smelling fresh. It was said by a Salcombe vicar that soldiers serving in China ended up with one of two things: a camphor chest, or a baby!

grow to spectacular sizes: the 80-year-old banana palms, the orange and lemon trees, the camphor and magnolias, including the vast *Magnolia Campbellii* planted in 1901, whose deep pink flowers burn into the hillside for a brief spell in late February/early March. At the other end of the season, in early autumn, don't miss the explosion of burning colour in the tender perennial borders. **Overbecks House and Garden ☎ 01548 842893, Youth Hostel ☎ 01548 842856.**

From Overbecks, continue down Courteney Drive past the wood-clad chalet-style Bolt Head Hotel to South Sands. To get back to the town, it is possible to walk along the shoreside road or take the South Sands Ferry to the ferry steps.

2. Soar Mill Cove to Burton Farm at Galmpton

From Soar Mill Cove take the coast path east towards Bolberry. There is quite a climb at first. At the top the path flattens out, offering fine views across to Dartmoor and Bigbury Bay. At Bolberry, walk through the National Trust car park. Cross the cattle grid with the Port Light to the left. Follow the road to the T-junction. Turn left. When the road forks, keep to the right, down the hill past Valley Cottage. After a short uphill climb, take the green tunnel footpath to the left. This emerges at a T-junction. Take a left (which seemingly leads to a private drive). On the right up some steps is a footpath to a stile. Walk diagonally left to a second stile. Burton Farm is now visible in the valley below. Follow the track to the farm.

Burton Farm

At this 15th-century working dairy and sheep farm in Galmpton, Ann Rossiter serves fabulous home-made food. A self-taught cook, Ann sources her food locally where she can: meat from Malcolm Patey at Harberton, vegetables from Wilton Farm at South Pool, and potatoes from Lidstone Farm just down the road at Galmpton. Milk and the clotted cream which smothers the scones comes from the farm dairy. Food is served in the conservatory, which looks out over the garden where there is an adventure play area, badminton and football posts. Burton Farm meets the needs of all ages: elderly aunts can watch the children larking outside whilst savouring steamed treacle pudding or Devonshire apple cake in the quiet and comfort of the dining room.

NB: A note for elderly aunts and small children: should the walk from Soar Mill Cove prove too taxing, Burton Farm is around a mile down the road from Malborough, from where there is a regular bus service to Kingsbridge and Salcombe. **Burton Farm, Galmpton ☎ 01548 561210.**

3. Salcombe to Gara Rock

(Five miles, with some uneven rocky ground.) This walk takes a route across the estuary and along a tree-lined carriage track to Gara Rock. The return trip follows the coast path around the estuary mouth back to East Portlemouth.

From the ferry steps at Salcombe, take the ferry to East Portle-mouth—note the **Venus Café** on the left at the top of the steps, which is great for ice creams and water for the dog. Turn right along the lane at the top of the steps or, if the tide is low, walk along the beach. Follow the road or beach to the National Trust car park. Turn left on to the track planted with lime trees. There is a steady climb up to Rickham, where the track ends at a lane. Take the footpath opposite through the old green tunnel of trees into an open field. Cross the stile, and turn right to the **Gara Rock Hotel** (closed at the time of writing). From here the coast path leads down to a delightfully sheltered beach with lots of rocks to climb, pools to explore and good swimming. Well worth the steep climb back up to the hotel. **Venus Café ☎ 01548 843558.**

To return to East Portlemouth, take the coast path which curves in front of the lookout. This leads back to East Portlemouth. As with most of this stretch of coast, there are some hairy moments and this way is not to be recommended for small or wild children, or nervous parents for that matter, but it is a surprisingly level walk—without switchback cliffs—for such a spectacular stretch of coastline. Along the way, listen to the stonechats: their distinctive call sounds like two pebbles being knocked together. Breathe the coconutty smell of the yellow gorse blossoms, and look out for tangles of bright pink 'spaghetti' over the bushes—a parasitic plant called dodder, which lives off the gorse. White bladder campion, tufty flowered thrift, wind-sculpted hawthorn and

THE CLEARANCES OF EAST PORTLEMOUTH

Now one of the most exclusive villages in which to own a house, East Portlemouth was in the last century a somewhat run down hamlet populated by sailors, fishermen and wreckers. Owned by the absent Duke of Cleveland, his agents informed him that as the villagers would not work the land properly and only cared for the sea, it was a needless expense to keep them as tenants. In something akin to the 18th and 19th century Highland Clearances, almost half the population was evicted and their cottages demolished, then the land was made into three large farms. In 1880 Portlemouth's plight came to the attention of the national press, and as a result the Duchess of Cleveland paid for the restoration of the parish church.

apple trees (from a walker's discarded apple core?) all show that despite harsh winds and salt spray, many plants thrive on the cliffland.

Scan the sea for dolphins, basking sharks and more commonly, gannets. Their strengthened 'crash helmet' skulls allow them to drop out of the sky kamikaze-style. Arriving back in Mill Bay, either follow the road, or if the tide is low, walk along the sand to return to the ferry.

St Winwalloe's Church, East Portlemouth, with its spectacular setting, deserves a visit before catching the ferry back to Salcombe. In the middle ages East Portlemouth was a significant port, with a flourishing ship-building industry. The village provided four ships and ninety men for the Crecy and Calais campaigns of 1346. It was wealth built up from this, as well as from fishing and farming, which funded the building of this fine fifteenth-century church, which is approached through a grave-yard scattered with the graves of shipwrecked mariners and smugglers. One eighteenth-century tombstone describes the murder of Richard Jarvis of Rickham by his apprentice girl, who was later burnt as a witch.

Sarah Fox, in her writings on the South Hams, recounts an occasion in the 1700s when a furious storm was raging in East Portlemouth. At the same time a funeral service was in full swing in the church. This was inter-rupted by word of a shipwreck in the raging sea below. The church was deserted in a flash, save for the lone coffin. Mourners and vicar had hurtled down the cliffs to plunder what they could from the stricken vessel.

Offshore—the Estuary

The Offshore section suggests ways of enjoying the Estuary and exploring the creeks between Salcombe and Kingsbridge.

The Kingsbridge-Salcombe Estuary stretches five miles, from Kingsbridge through Salcombe to the coast at Bolt Head. It is not a true estuary, but rather a series of flooded river plains, its narrow winding creeks extending to the most unspoilt and secluded countryside. The estuary and foreshore is a Site of Special Scientific Interest (SSSI), the water being clear, sheltered and salty. It provides a rare environment for underwater plants and animals. Bird and marine life is diverse and prolific. Because of the exceptionally sheltered and saline conditions, some species have been found here at their most northerly recorded point. Beneath the mud are rare and extraordinary sea slugs and snails; one particular slug is so rare it remains unnamed.

HUMAN BAIT

An effective bait for trying to get those crabs and shrimps out from under the rocks is the human hand. Put your hand in the water, be very still and patient and wait. Soon, the curious inhabitants will venture out to investigate and feed off those delicious dead skin cells on your hand.

Taking to the Water

Rivermaid The Rivermaid passenger boat runs between Salcombe and Kingsbridge (tides permitting). Estuary cruises are available at certain times around high tide. These go between Salcombe and Kingsbridge, around the creeks or, weather permitting, around the coast either side of Salcombe harbour. **Rivermaid ☎ 01548 853607.**

Sea Fishing Skipper Kevin Rowe takes groups out mackerel fishing. The two-hour trips run daily during the season. Kevin is very patient and good with children, all fishing tackle is supplied, and you can keep what you catch.

Half and full day trips are available for the more serious angler. Under Kevin Rowe's guidance you would hope to catch cod, ling, pollack or whiting. **Tightlines ☎ 01548 843818.**

Boat Hire Another option is to be independent and hire a boat from one of the several companies in Salcombe which offer this. Exploring the creeks at leisure allows more time for really discovering the places for yourself. Check the tide times before you do so, because much of the estuary is inaccessible at low tide, when 450 hectares of mud are exposed. You'll need a chart of the estuary, a tide table, and be sure to pick up an information leaflet from the Harbour Office at Whitestrand, which clearly delivers the do's and don'ts of the estuary.

Houseboats Another way of getting to know the ria (a glacial water-filled valley) is by staying on it: houseboats are available for hire, moored in the peace and shelter of 'the bag'—some ten minutes from the harbour by launch. The houseboats offer a different perspective to a holiday in Salcombe. Tides and light structure your days, and learning how to leap between boats and tie knots is an adventure in itself—not to mention the heron-watching at dawn, and being left utterly undisturbed. Contact **The Salcombe Houseboat Holidays ☎ 01548 843730**.

Sailing

From the entrance over the Salcombe Bar, all the way up to Kingsbridge, the Estuary offers sheltered water for sailing and boating, and is ideal for learning to sail. The Island Cruising Club—founded in 1951 by a group of sailing enthusiasts on a co-operative basis—has grown into one of the leading sailing holiday and Royal Yachting Association schools. The operation is run from a converted Mersey ferry ('Egremont'), which is permanently moored in the estuary.

Sailing at Salcombe

Residential and non-residential courses are run for all age groups, with up to fifty residents staying on board. During school holidays, children over ten can attend a cadet week, where sailing is just part of the fun. The ICC also hires out dinghies, and keelboats to experienced sailors.

Winter Sailing Invest in a good wetsuit and enrol on a winter course, for in winter the estuary is wonderfully empty, course fees considerably less, and there's so much space to learn in.

Cadet Courses Take advantage of living locally: enrol your children in the excellent cadet courses run for local members by both the ICC and the Salcombe Yacht Club. **Island Cruising Club ☎ 01548 843481. Salcombe Yacht Club ☎ 01548 842593.**

Exploring the Creeks

Creek- and estuary-side villages are awkward to reach by road, because of having to follow an unwieldy route around the estuary, but a joy to visit by water (tides permitting).

Frogmore (or lake of frogs) heads a creek of the same name which is accessible by boat, one and a half hours either side of high water. This allows time to moor up and take a creekside walk. At low tide, walk along the foreshore to the pair of restored lime kilns; alternatively, follow the road taking the footpath to the left past the Globe Inn opposite, which leads to the shore. As well as burning limestone with coal and furze to turn it into lime to improve the acidic local soils, this kiln served to cook the village's Sunday pot roasts—the oven built into the wall is still visible.

Follow the footpath above the foreshore, with fine views of the creeks. In winter, this is one of the best places to spot wading birds and ducks wintering here from the arctic and Scandinavia. From here there is a choice: to retrace steps, or to take a longer circular route through West Charleton village and along an old turnpike road back to Frogmore. This walk is described in detail in the Coast and Countryside Service's Salcombe–Kingsbridge Estuary Walks leaflet, which offers six easy walks around the estuary.

TIDES

Be aware of tides—invest in a tide table. Rivers and beaches are transformed by the different states of the tide. Low tide is the time to go rockpooling—on a moonlit night you'll see the limpets moving about! Birds and fish populate the foreshore mud of the estuary at low tide.

GREENSHANK BAY

For me, Frogmore Creek means 'Greenshank Bay' and 'Diving Duck Reach', not to be found on the OS map. From Frogmore village follow the public footpath along the north side of the creek for about half a mile. Turn past the saltmarsh at Cleevehouse Bay, until the path and creek bend to the west. Across the creek is Greenshank Bay. As the rising tide covers the mud, greenshanks gather. They can appear almost white, their legs greenish-grey, their slender bills slightly upturned. At low tide, greenshanks work the shallows of the creeks, sometimes running through the water for tiny oppossum shrimps. They stay all year round on the Kingsbridge estuary, which boasts more resident greenshanks than any other English estuary.

Further downstream, a long reach curves round towards Halwell Wood on the southern shore. I call this deep water channel 'Diving Duck Reach'. It is rich in fish, crustaceans and other estuary invertebrates. Lowest tide reveals a forest of tube worms, orange sponges and grey sea squirts living in the mud at the water's edge. Goldeneye duck are common here, and red-breasted mergansers can often be seen diving in synchronised succession.

Ever since great crested grebes returned to nest at Slapton in 1973, some have come across to the estuary. They travel great distances underwater, and dive frequently, so it can be difficult to keep track of them. The little grebe, or dabchick, with powder puff stumpy tail, also winters here. As the tide begins to fall they dive among the floating seaweeds along the shore. In summer the only diving ducks are the flotillas of baby shelduck. The black and white adult shelduck are beautiful, but they can't dive. They nest in old rabbit burrows under the gorse bushes on Ham Point. In late May or early June the parents bring their brood—a straggling crocodile of about twelve fluffy black and grey ducklings down to the creek. In contrast to their parents, these pied cotton wool balls can dive at will, bobbing up with a shake of their tiny heads.

Try to include a visit to **The Globe Inn**, a friendly pub which is very welcoming to children. **The Globe Inn** ☎ **01548 531351.**

Frogmore Bakery Down the road is **Frogmore Bakery**, famous for its home-baked granary bread and doughnuts. By 5 am, bakers John Eaton and Alistair Carter are well into their morning's work. Sacks of strong white, stoneground, wholemeal, and rye flour are piled almost to the ceiling of this small village bakery. As much as 40 kilos can be used in a day. A tub, big enough to swim in, 'develops' a load of flour, fresh yeast, salt and water ready for proving, while Alistair and John work fast and with an economy of movement essential in the pressing heat of the bread oven.

The thud, cut and knead of dough marks a rhythm as John scales a batch of wholemeal loaves. Alistair meanwhile works his way through a tray of pasties, deftly scalloping their pastry edges. Then a sudden whoosh of even hotter air blasts as the cast iron oven door is opened and amber loaves are scooped out with a long handled wooden peal and left to rest.

There has been a bakery on this site in Frogmore for 130 years, and I doubt if much has changed in either the baking process or the ingredients used since the 1870s. Very little is automated, right down to the hand-operated jam squirter for filling the doughnuts. Loaves are individually cut and shaped. Pastries, scones, buns and croissants are all made by hand.

Frogmore Bakery has been in John's family since 1976. His father Andrew retired from baking a while ago but still manages the village stores. John was joined by Alistair, an experienced chef, ten years ago. Between them they bring a broad and detailed understanding of bread and pastry making. How long bakeries such as Frogmore can survive is very much in question. They already find themselves struggling with the demands of recent health and safety regulations, and in order to comply with these have had to stop making some of their most popular pies.

CROOKED CHIMNEYS

When you're next in Frogmore or West Charleton, watch out for crooked chimneys. Did you know that you can use them as a compass? For they face towards the prevailing south-westerly wind. But why? Because the lime mortar used in their construction has expanded on the damp side away from the drying action of the wind, thus pushing the chimney in a south-westerly direction.

SALTMARSH PLANTS

Downstream of the stepping stones at the head of South Pool Creek is a fringe of saltmarsh, and even a saltmarsh island which grows a little more each year. In summer there is a fascinating progression of saltmarsh vegetation. There is something otherworldly about saltmarsh plants. First to grow out of the bare mud are upright succulents, resembling miniature branched cacti—without the spines. This is glasswort (*Salicornia spp.*), so called for its early use in glass making—the plants were burnt and their ash added to sand in a furnace. Once glasswort has established itself around the outer edge of the saltmarsh, other plants follow: sea-plantain, sea arrow grass and saltmarsh grass all grow in South Pool, along with the delicate pink flowering sea-spurrey and sea-milkwort. In late summer the mauve daisy flower heads of the sea aster with their yellow centres stand tall above the brimming water.

By opening time at 9 am, the day's baking is complete, and outside the village store a small group of customers have gathered. I realise how rare and precious the smell of fresh hand-baked bread is in our villages, and how the skills of bakers like John and Andrew could so easily be lost. **Frogmore Village Stores and Bakery ☎ 01548 531236.**

Frogmore Regatta The timing of the Frogmore regatta is dependent upon the times of high tide. Gloriously set on fields which flank the head of the creek, Frogmore Regatta is a laid-back event and tremendous fun. A donkey derby, rowing races, ram roast & cream teas combine to make a Saturday afternoon in early August disappear quite delightfully. Having browsed at the odd craft or produce stall, grab yourself a hay bale and something cooling to sip, and settle in to idle away an hour or two beside the water, watching others paddling furiously around the creek. Meanwhile there are children's races to exhaust the kids, and if competitions aren't their thing, there's plenty of field to charge about in. And you can enjoy the privilege of a trip up the creek for around £1.

South Pool

South Pool sits at the head of another idyllic creek. By water, this remote village is accessible for only an hour either side of high tide. Until comparatively recently, the village was virtually self-sufficient. Doreen Shepherd describes the traditional way of life in her book *South Pool: Portrait of a South Devon Village in the mid-twentieth century* (available in local shops). At that time, the village had its own school, church, chapel and shop—which was supplemented by a collection of visiting shops, including butcher Cleave (a farmer from Slapton, whose meat swung from hooks on his horse and cart); baker Seymour from Chillington, and Messrs Rudd and Prin from Dartmouth with their suitcases full of underwear. The visiting hairdresser was Mr Alf Moore from Beesands, but the permanent wave was (appropriately) the job of Mr Lenny Crimp of Kingsbridge.

Mains water and electricity were only introduced in 1949; before then, water was channelled from springs or surface streams into communal taps, which are still in place: at the top of the village opposite Mole Hill, and at Cliff's End. There is also one remaining water pump in Herring Street. You might well pass by a horse mount, a cart swing, a buddle hole for water drainage, a mangold hold and a milk stand. There is also mention of the light on the bridge, donated by a certain Mrs Halifax 'to enable her son, Gerald, who was given to heavy drinking sessions at the nearby Union Inn, to walk safely over the bridge to the house she had previously had built for him named Albert Cottage.'

Times changed. In 1968 the school closed, closely followed by the shop. In 1972 the post office closed and the Western National Bus service was withdrawn. Today, the gorgeous setting and collection of traditional thatch and stone cottages has made it prey to the tourist industry, with around sixty percent of houses being holiday homes. **The Millbrook Inn** is busy and boaty, and serves good meals. Either side of high tide are the busiest times. To avoid the crush, why not linger a while in the village; visit the fourteenth-century church with its 16th century screens painted with the story of St Nicholas, and carved with the head of a grotesque one-eyed imp above the pulpit. The network of green lanes and bridlepaths around the village make for some glorious walks. **The Millbrook Inn ☎ 01548 531581.**

A BEGINNER'S GUIDE TO SAILING

With such a varied coastline and beautiful tidal estuaries, the South Hams offers lots of opportunities for sailing at all levels, and the tidal Salcombe Estuary is ideal for gaining experience.

James and Victoria Hannaford (age 18 and 16 respectively) from East Allington are both cadets at Salcombe Yacht Club. James now has his own boat and competes at weekends during the season. He hopes when he finishes university to sail around Britain. Below are James and Victoria's tips for those wishing to give sailing a try.

For Visitors

The Island Cruising Club in Salcombe has been teaching people to sail for over 50 years. A RYA-recognised sail training centre, students are assured professional teaching of the highest quality and standards. Students are taught in small groups and have lots of individual tuition. The ICC is geared up to teach all ages at all levels. They particularly welcome beginners. **Island Cruising Club ☎ 01548 531176. www.icc-salcombe.co.uk.**

SPEAK THE LANGUAGE

Starboard – right
Port – left
Bow – front
Stern – back
Mainsail – the big sail
Jib – the small sail at the front.
Spinnaker – bigger than the jib, smaller than the mainsail
'Water' (shouted) – Get out of my way!
Painter – rope

For Locals

Tuesday nights from May to September is when the cadets at Salcombe Yacht club meet. Members have the opportunity to learn to sail off Small's Cove in the club's own Laser Picos and Toppers. Parents have fun helping out in the rescue boats. The teaching is quite informal and the more experienced cadets help the beginners. Once ready for racing, there are cadet classes in the Saturday racing programme in the season. There are lots of social events for all members at the club and a good bar. And after the evening sail on a Tuesday, cadets can order sausage and chips at the clubhouse which offers grandstand views of the estuary from its terrace. ☎ 01548 842593 www.salcombeyc.org.uk.

Cadet classes are also available at the **Royal Dart Yacht Club, Dartmouth ☎ 01803 752704 www.royaldart.co.uk,** and **Dittisham Sailing Club, email c.a.taylor@ex.ac.uk.**

The Gear

- Buoyancy aid—nothing too bulky, and be sure to get one which provides support to the neck.
- Long wet suit for chilly days
- Flat-bottomed shoes with grip, or wet suit boots.
- If you're doing a lot of sailing, hands can get sore from the ropes. Specialist gloves are available and save blisters.
- A Tide Table

Where to get it

- **The Salcombe Boat Store** in Island Street provides helfpul assistance from experienced sailors and has a wide range of clothes and equipment, new and second-hand.
- **Wills Marine** in Kingsbridge is mostly for surfers, but has a good selection for sailors.

TIDES AT SALCOMBE

Unsure if the tide is going in or out? Look at a boat out to sea. If the bow is turning to the mouth of the harbour, the tide is coming in. If the stern is facing the harbour, the tide is going out. This is a pretty reliable guide unless the wind is very strong.

Kingsbridge

Kingsbridge serves as the market town for many outlying villages in the South Hams. Shops in and around Fore Street reflect the diverse needs of the rural community, and the local calendar is peppered with agricultural events.

KIngsbridge Town Judging from the fine views of the estuary seen from the top of the hill in Fore Street, it might be assumed that, like Salcombe, life in Kingsbridge focuses on the water. Not so, for surrounded as it is by soft rolling hills and fertile valleys, where small mixed farms continue to be the lifeblood of the community, Kingsbridge remains the vital centre for these small villages as it has done since mediæval times. There are many and varied routes into the town from the small villages which surround it: Buckland-Tout-Saints, Bowcombe, West Alvington, Churchstow, West Charleton and The Mounts, to name but a few.

The town is a typically Saxon shape, with houses facing the central spine of Fore Street, behind which lie narrow strips of land known as 'burghage plots'. Small passageways to the east and west of Fore Street meander through to the two main outer passageways: Eastern Backway and Western Backway, both of which follow the course of the old mill leats. The eastern leat from the River Dod has been culverted underground, whilst the western leat still runs its course along the end of the gardens, where large blue slate stones form bridges across the water. Squeezebelly Lane is one of a number of charming passageways; as its name suggests, it challenges the wider form. In wandering around these back lanes which thread their way down to the leats to the east and west of Fore Street, notice the local slates, called 'shiners', which are put to all kinds of uses, including flagstones, wall copings, tombstones and paving stones. The decorative tiles hanging on the upper stories of some of the houses in the town are a further use of blue slate. It was hung as a cladding mainly as a protection against the weather, being quarried locally at Sunnydale, on the coast near Beesands, at Buckland-Tout-Saints, and Molescombe near Frogmore. The

Kingsbridge from the estuary

King of Prussia pub at the bottom of Fore Street has its slates arranged in a fish scale pattern around a curved outer wall which was shaped to allow carriages to negotiate the corner successfully.

The older gates, railings and bollards of Kingsbridge have a distinctive style characteristic of Lidstones, the local foundry, which also manufactured its own kitchen ranges. Most locals had a Lidstone; they were exported in great numbers to Newfoundland (through the 'cod' connection), where they can still be seen working today. They also manufactured tools and iron work for shipyards.

Farming and tourism are the main industries around Kingsbridge. In summer it isn't unusual for whole families to move into caravans so they can let out their homes to the holiday trade. On Saturdays, armies of cleaners pour out of the villages into the holiday houses for frantic change-overs. However, with the coming of September, a quiet descends upon the South Hams. Gone are the choked roads of July and August. It's a time when locals reclaim the beaches and enjoy the last of the summer. It's also the time for fruits. Local apples start to appear on sale, field mushrooms give reason for early morning walks, and blackberries taste all the better for the scratches earned whilst picking them.

Starting with the Kingsbridge Show, and moving on to harvest celebrations, this is a busy time of year.

Kingsbridge Show The Kingsbridge Agricultural and Horticultural Society hold the annual Kingsbridge Show on the first Saturday in September. The local community turns out in force for a day packed with events, demonstrations, and entertainment of one form or another. The edge of competition is in the air as the modest prizes are hard fought for. Trade stands are packed with local businesses offering

Tiling patterns in Fore Street / 'Shiners' bridging the leat in Western Backway / White Hart Passage

discounts on this and that, the food tent draws the curious and the hungry, and the craft tent is a great place to buy early for Christmas. For a moment's respite, visit the horticulture and homecraft tent and gasp at the wondrous leeks, heady dahlias, and fairytale cabbages. Then ponder upon 'the most humorous boiled egg, with or without accessories'. Rounding off the afternoon is the young farmers' tug-of-war, with brawny teams heaving ropes back and forth until one side finally collapses. **Kingsbridge Show, Borough Farm (off the A381 approximately 2 miles north of Kingsbridge).**

Harvest Festival It's well worth noting the dates of harvest festivals in nearby churches (East Allington, West Alvington, South Milton, Churchstow, Loddiswell), for this is one time of the year when churches are certain to be buzzing. The celebration of Harvest Festival remains an important marker in the lives of local village communities, who put on magnificent spreads at harvest suppers held in village and church halls up and down the South Hams. The churches are

Kingsbridge Show

bountiful, with arrangements of fruit, vegetables, corn, barley, hops and flowers—a far cry from my own suburban memories of the sixties, when harvest festival amounted to stacks of canned vegetables topped with an apple or two.

Fatstock Another important date in the agricultural calendar is mid-December, when butchers shut up shop to come to the Kingsbridge Fatstock show. Beautiful beasts are brought to market to compete for much sought-after prizes. Farmers turn out in their best tweeds, and there's a lot of talking and dealing to be done. Until recently, it was the time for the Christmas fowl to be shown and sold; this is still the case in Dartmouth, which holds its fatstock show in the market square.

Devon Honey David Wilson, the Secretary of the South Hams Beekeepers' Club, is the largest honey producer in the South Hams. From his home in Sherford he keeps 70 hives—producing, in a good year, up to two tons of honey. In honey circles, they say that out of ten years, two are good, two are bad, and six around average. The unpredictable Devon weather makes or breaks the beekeeper.

David Wilson has lived near Kingsbridge for most of his life, and he remembers the time when most farmers kept bees (in straw skeps), not so much for their honey as for pollinating crops. They were invaluable in the apple and cherry orchards, and in the strawberry fields. Changes in the South Devon landscape have affected the honey bee: the disappearance of the elm, with its early flowering pollen-drenched catkins which were a valuable source of food, as were the hay meadows with spring grazing; and a hay cut in June allowed flowering plants to set seed, thus maintaining a high diversity of species. Thankfully the hedgerows remain intact, providing excellent and varied forage for bees.

On the first Monday and Tuesday in August, the South Hams Beekeepers' Club holds its annual exhibition in Kingsbridge, market hall. It's a hive of information.

BUZZ WORDS

For instance, did you know:
- For every pound of honey, bees make eight million visits to a flower.
- Bees fly the equivalent of two and a half times round the world for a pound of honey. And all for around £2.70 a jar!

Local honey is available from: Nicholson's Wholefood and Health Shop, 12 Fore St Kingsbridge ☎ 01548 854347; Healthwise, 81 Fore St, Kingsbridge ☎ 01548 857707. David Wilson's honey is on sale at Hope Cove Post Office ☎ 01548 561249, Frogmore Bakery & General Stores ☎ 01548 531236, and Chillington Post Office ☎ 01548 580371.

Kingsbridge

The joy of Kingsbridge is that it has maintained its small scale, and has thus largely resisted the arrival of high street chains. Shops are largely local businesses, and you can do virtually all your shopping in Fore Street. Kingsbridge is a no-nonsense centre, with functional, practical shops providing good service. Everyday needs are a priority.

Practical needs
Nicola's Do you remember those pleated polythene rain hats? Or those plastic macs which packed into a small poppered wallet? Nicola's might well stock them. They might stock anything, for stuffed into a small space are all manner of goods. This is the joy of Nicola's, from the joke plastic biscuit to swimsuits, jigsaws, ladies' skirts, and some very good sailing shoes and sandals. So, if there's something you've been on the lookout for, it's worth a try. **Nicola's, 74 Fore Street ☎ 01548 852248.**

John H Donovan and Son
If you ask John Donovan 'the fourth' (the present owner of Donovan's China, Glass and Furnishing Warehouse) for an anti-macassar, he won't bat an eyelid. It's

their business to stock just about anything for the home—they even sell cup and curtain hooks individually! They've been in existence since 1873, and in their present premises since the end of the 19th century.

Donovan's caters for a stack of domestic needs. In the front of the shop is the china section, in the middle, linen, and in the back, kitchenware. Carpets and furniture are upstairs. I searched heaven and earth for fly strips, eventually finding them in Donovan's kitchen department, along with cotton mop heads—in all weights. A well-run family business; the next Donovan to take the reins will be Hazel 'the first'. **Donovan's, 49 Fore Street ☎ 01548 852342.**

Nonsuch Hanging on the rails of Nonsuch, a small clothes shop at the lower end of Fore Street, is the

'Muddy Puddles' range of children's waterproof clothing. Tough and durable, this very practical and colourful outdoor gear has been designed by someone who knows her mud—farmer Susie Cullen of Ringmore. What began as a purely waterproof collection has grown to include wellie socks, bold 'digger mad' and 'tractor mad' tee shirts for enthusiasts, and useful cotton boiler suits and fleeces at affordable prices. Ideal for outdoor-loving kids, Muddy Puddles clothes are available by mail order. **Nonsuch, 13 Fore Street ☎ 01548 852892. Muddy Puddles, Hingston Farm, Bigbury, Kingsbridge ☎ 01548 810477.**

One third of your body heat is lost through your head, so it makes sense to get a hat. Why not pop into **Milburns**, which is stuffed with sensible practical outdoor gear, and buy one of Claire McKillop's fleece hats. These colourful titfers are inexpensive and gloriously cosy. Children love the large paw-print designs. Claire McKillop also makes fleece scarves and neckwarmers from her workshop in town. **Milburns, 22 Fore Street ☎ 01548 853926. www.artandmystery.co.uk**

Kingsbridge

A short walk from Fore Street in Wallingford Road is **Countrywest Trading** (formerly West Devon and Cornwall Farmers). Don't be daunted by those fearfully capable women seen tearing into the car park in huge muddy vehicles and loading up with sacks of feed, seed and weed (killer). Farming women don't hang about: their days, like their fields, are very productive. There are still plenty of working farmhouse kitchens round and about, churning out huge quantities of home-cooked food, dispatching cakes this way and that, and filling shelves with jams, chutneys and jellies. As well as being a great place to browse, it is a lifeline for many people who live around Kingsbridge. It specialises in pet and animal supplies, wellies and serious rain gear, riding garb, all kinds of tools. There's no pussyfooting around with small quantities here: string comes by the mile and seed by the pound. Bunches of seedlings on sale give a helpful nudge to the inexperienced grower as to what goes in when. **Countrywest Trading, Wallingford Road** ☎ 01548 857321. Directions: Turn right at the top of Fore Street into Duncombe Street. At the first crossroads, turn left

into Wallingford Road (look out for the vegetable stall in someone's front garden). **Countrywest Trading** is about 100 yards along on the left.

Harbour Bookshop

Whether it's a book or a card you're looking for, the odds are that the Harbour Bookshop has just the thing. For this small bookshop is thoughtfully stocked with browsable books in manageable numbers. and a discerning selection of greetings cards. Helpful staff are always on hand to give advice and information, and they can get hold of books for you in a trice. **The Harbour Bookshop, 2 Mill Street** ☎ 01548 857233.

Salters Bookshelf

There is no fear of running out of holiday reading matter for, like the Salcombe branch, Salters in Kingsbridge has devoted considerable shelf space to a book exchange. There is also a good selection of general (new) reading matter, and particularly fine local interest books, maps and

charts. And aside from a distracting collection of old postcards there are some good old-fashioned jigsaws for those rainy days. **Salter's Bookshelf, 89 Fore Street** ☎ 01548 844464

Gifts
Elements

Pretty and fresh, Elements lightens up the corner which joins Mill Street to Fore Street, with Cath Kidston pastels and flowery prints, the firm blue and white stripes of Cornishware, and icecream colours of the enamelware. Upon entering this small store, note the detailed applique 'open' sign on the door. This is the work of local art teacher and textile artist Emma Charleton. More of her applique pictures are on the walls—assemblies of tiny maps of the Salcombe

Vegetable stall in Wallingford Road / Elements in Fore Street

Kingsbridge

estuary with fragments of printed cotton delicately stitched and minute shells or stones or paper. Also hung on the walls are limited edition prints of the paintings of local artist Joyce Houghton, and the elegant landscape photography of Mick Allen. Off the wall are the exuberant lampshades—which could be mistaken for Audrey Hepburn's hat collection—from the Oxford-based makers Ruby and Pearl, whose love of flounces, polka dots and floaty ostrich feather trims provides a welcome antidote to minimalism.
Elements
4 Fore Street
☎ **01548 854343**

Pig Finca
'Items for happy living and an easy frame of mind'. Angus and Sally Ann, founders of Pig Finca, planned to live in Spain; they even had a place lined up there called Pig Finca. Plans changed, and instead they opened a shop in Fore Street of the same name. Bringing some of that Spanish sensuality to a rural market town has proved an unlikely but successful move. Current owner Liz Lee continues the tradition of stocking 'things I like'. These include an eclectic selection of music, north

African ceramics, natural paint pigments, and a small collection of clothes. Then there are the 'blow ins': gaudy tin trays, hand-made soap, exotic hair clips and clunky plastic fly curtains which come and go, giving locals the perfect excuse for repeated visits. The Pig Finca footprint has made its way down the hill to the Pig Finca Café—see Eating Out. **Pig Finca, 105 Fore Street ☎ 01548 854221.**

Two markets
WI Market 'Local produce for local people' is the catchphrase for the hugely successful WI markets held weekly in 500 locations throughout Britain: an annual turnover of £11 million is an awful lot of cakes. It's a sophisticated business, and quality control is firm. In Kingsbridge on Wednesday mornings, a small queue gathers beneath the town hall

clock as it approaches 8.15. They are mainly regulars, awaiting the pick of the bunch, including cut flowers from the garden (lilies of the valley, bluebells and delightful arrangements of seasonal flowers). The selection of perennials is unusual, and fresh produce is quickly snapped up. The crafts, although a little heavy on the knitting side, have some exquisite pressed flower greetings cards, as well as hand-sewn ones.
Whatever is on sale at the WI market, you can be sure it's of the finest quality, complying with guidelines right down to the screw-top lid. Freshness is carefully monitored: sponges and savouries must be cooked the day before or on the day of sale, and fruit cakes by the beginning of the week. Unsold cakes and pies do not reappear. Incidentally, the WI market is one of the

Women's Institute market

Kingsbridge

organisation's few activities in which men are included, as they may sell their produce. Certainly men are keen customers—and often head the queue at the pie and cake stall. WI Country Markets Hamper Scheme is a super gift idea in which a hamper filled with goodies local to the recipient is delivered to their door. ☎ 01189 394646 for details. WI Market, Town Hall, Wednesday 8.30 am–12.30 pm.

Farmers' Market On the first Saturday of each month between 10 am and 2 pm in Kingsbridge town square (at the head of the estuary, adjoining the Quay Car Park) is the Farmers' Market. This provides an opportunity for local people to buy local produce from a local source, including chocolate, cheese, chillies, meat, vegetables, eggs and fudge.

Things To Do in Kingsbridge

The Quayside Leisure Centre There is a 25-metre swimming pool at Quayside Leisure Centre and a shallow one for non-swimmers. The centre organises lots of activities throughout the year with all manner of children's activities at half terms and holidays. There are squash courts for hire, a sports hall, a dance studio, and a well equipped exercise room. **Quayside Leisure Centre** ☎ 01548 857100.

The Reel Cinema Kingsbridge is lucky to have its own small independent cinema. The Reel Cinema is housed in the Town Hall at the top of Fore Street. It plays mainly first run films, along with the odd classic or art film. Many locals meet up in the café before or after a movie, taking advantage of the 'Reel Meal Deal' (food and a film). **The Reel Cinema Information Line** ☎ 01548 856636 www.thereelcinema.co.uk

Harbour House A community-based centre for the arts and yoga, situated opposite the Tourist Information Centre on the Quay. It houses art and craft exhibitions and runs regular yoga, craft

and art classes. Upstairs is a vegetarian café (see Eating Out) There is also a large well-lit room on the first floor which is available for hire. **Harbour House, The Promenade, Kingsbridge.**

Coronation Park A short walk from the Quay car park, across the road which runs along the embankment, lies Coronation Park. This small, old-fashioned recreation ground offers what a park should: swings and slides, a putting green, tennis courts, a small café with tables and chairs outside; and if you're lucky, cream-clad ladies and gentlemen clunking the afternoon away on the trimmed bowling green.

The Cookworthy Museum Housed in the old grammar school at the top of Fore Street is the

South Devon Chilli Farm stall, Farmers' Market / Kingsbridge Town Hall

Kingsbridge

Cookworthy Museum of Rural Life. Recent restoration of the seventeenth-century school building (with the later Victorian headmaster's house attached) has transformed the school into a sequence of airy exhibition spaces. The school hall, complete with imposing headmaster's desk and chair carved with the names of boys gone by, is home to an exhibition of the story of Kingsbridge. Local geology—the first exhibit—outlines the complexities of the many-decked geological sandwich which forms South Devon. This is clearly and simply portrayed through maps and clear text, and helpful samples of mica schist, green schist, meadfoot bed and Dartmoor slate. Many of the exhibits can be touched, and all are quite without superfluous 'gizmos'.

Also in the Museum is **Balkwill's Pharmacy**, with its countless pots, jars, tins and drawers of seeds, roots, leaves and powders. Browsing here may evoke familiar feelings for some.

Downstairs is the kitchen, with its local Burgoyne range. This room is filled with Victorian domestic gadgets and equipment. Outside are kibblers, cutters, crushers and bruisers—a complete collection of local farm implements from the 1920s and 30s, grouped together by season. Also downstairs is a comfortable new viewing gallery which allows virtual access to exhibits in parts of this many staired seventeenth century building which were previously out of bounds to the less mobile visitor. The garden is also used for occasional 'special days' when local skills and crafts are demonstrated. Keep an eye out for these. Another important date is the Thursday after Easter—family day again, with lots of opportunity to learn about rural skills, and when the children make flower baskets with the help of the local flower club. Also at the Cookworthy is a local Heritage Resource Centre, which is open throughout the year. **Cookworthy Museum, 108 Fore Street** ☎ **01548 853235.**

Just up the road from the museum, tucked behind 112 Fore Street is the **Kingsbridge Community Garden**, an acre of walled garden on sloping ground, which for years remained neglected and overgrown. Ten years hard work by a core of local volunteer gardeners, fundraisers and supporters have transformed it into a productive, organic community garden with all kinds of different growing areas to enjoy. There's a bog garden, a dry garden for Mediterranean plants, a fruit cage, lots of raised beds growing rare salad varieties, vegetables and flowers. Tender plants and seedlings are nurtured inside polytunnels whilst more invasive species are planted within the confines of recycled rubber tyres.

The garden is a kind of living experiment and is certainly the place for getting ideas on how to do things in simple and inexpensive ways. Terraces are constructed with sleepers, fixed in place by whatever wood is to hand, and garden structures are made from willow grown on site. An efficient composting system has been constructed by two local lads from scrap wood and carpet pieces, and next to

Volunteers working in the Community Garden

Kingsbridge

the compost is the squirmy wormery. Growing towers (with in-built watering systems) are made from pig wire, rubbish bags and lengths of pierced hose, and even the loo is self-composting.

Over the years the scrub and brambles have been cleared to make way for more growing space as the garden has edged its way down the hill. The planting of a tranquil area is underway at the lower end. Once this has been established the acre of garden will be under control, and the team can relax a bit and enjoy the fruits of their labour. But now there are murmurs about clearing the scrub beyond the boundary wall—which currently acts as a repository for discarded fridges and washing machines.

Do take some time to drop in and take a look at this remarkable garden, or if you want to get involved look at the website for contact details. Plants and produce are for sale on site or at Kingsbridge farmers market on the first Saturday in the month. Opening hours 8.30 am–5.00 pm weekdays. **Kingsbridge Community Garden, 112 Fore Street www.-kingsbridgegarden.co.uk.**

Eating Out

Have you ever found yourself on holiday with children, trawling the streets in the early evening for something to eat, only to find yourself in that hungry gap when daytime cafés are closed, and evening eateries are only at the potato peeling stage? Kingsbridge is exceptionally well off for child-friendly eating places, where one can either eat in or take away, with good, reasonably priced food before 7.30 pm.

Giovanni's Italians have a way with children, and Giovanni's is no exception. A visit here is always an occasion: children are treated like adults, and waited on with aplomb. Details like personal pepper-grinding and parmesan sprinkling make it a little special, not to mention the 'real' chips, and authentic in-a-stemmed-glass prawn cocktails. But don't let child-free readers be put off. Open by 6.30 pm, this family restaurant in Church Street turns out a magnificent spaghetti, as well as more elaborate Italian dishes. **Giovanni's, Church Street ☎ 01548 856707.**

Portlemouth Pastries
Comfort food at its best: Portlemouth Pastries sells fine British pies, cakes and tray bakes. They offer the definitive treacle tart, a very Devon cider cake, and their pasties take some beating. If you're feeling adventurous, the almond and apricot pie takes the biscuit. **Portlemouth Pastries, 15 Church Street ☎ 01548 854073.**

Red Earth Deli
Everything is handpicked at this small deli at the bottom of Fore Street. Ideal for assembling a rather special lunch: fragrant hams, chorizos and pastramis as well as real scotch eggs and filling pies. The olive and pickle counter is a help yourself affair, and the cheese a thoughtful mix of local and continental. There is an opportunity to try some of the delicacies in the restful coffee bar (with daily papers and brown leather sofas), which serves a particularly sustaining chocolate brownie. **Red Earth Deli ☎ 01548 856100. www.redearthdeli.co.uk**

James Marshall outside Red Earth Deli

Kingsbridge

Ken's Kitchen—Fish and Chips is known for the generous size of its portions. On sunny days, a take-away can be enjoyed in the small public space (next to the bingo hall), above what was Dodbrooke cattle market. The raised walkway allowed farmers to view the cattle in the pens below. Children love to sit upon the carved wooden animals, bag of chips in hand. **Ken's Kitchen, Church Street.**

The Dodbrooke Inn A friendly pub, serving inexpensive home-cooked meals—again, fish and chips a speciality, as are charcoal-grilled steaks. Sunday roasts are inexpensive and popular. Food is served from 7 pm, and families are welcome. **The Dodbrooke Inn, Church Street ☎ 01548 852068.**

Mange Tout When you've trekked all the way up to the top of Fore Street, pick up a deserved treat at this excellent little deli. Great for gathering ingredients for that special picnic from a fine range of meats, cheeses, patés and pies, complemented by moist cakes and wicked gateaux. The sandwiches are excellent—great combinations between the freshest of bread.

These may be taken away or eaten in, for Mange Tout has a small café at the rear of the shop; but the high stools make it difficult to accommodate small children or those with disabilities. Outside, on the other hand, there is a small courtyard with tables and chairs. **Mange Tout, 84 Fore Street ☎ 01548 852133.**

The Mahabharat Balti House Not for the hard of hearing, this robust and popular establishment serves the 'after the pub' crowd, as well as parties. Early evening is time for the quiet meal for two. A definite plus is the 'bring your own' drink policy, with no corkage to pay. For those whose teeth are set on edge by the iron dishes, take-aways are available; free delivery within a five-mile radius for orders over £25.00. In Kingsbridge, free delivery for orders over £15.00. **Mahabharat Balti House, 7a Mill Street ☎ 01548 857072.**

Support your Local Crisp Burts Potato Chips is a small business based at the Parcel Shed in Station Yard. At the turn of the century, when the Parcel Shed was used to send primroses, snowdrops, live rabbits and other fresh produce to London, the

crisped chip was a rare luxury—indeed the fried potato had only recently become acceptable as part of the British diet. It was the invention of the mechanical potato peeler in the 1920s that made the crisp commercially possible. Local potatoes are hand-fried in sunflower oil (the name of the frier is stamped on the packet), then flavoured with sea salt, mature cheddar, hot chilli and lemon, or just left plain. These hand-made crisps can be found on the shelves of local garages, Mange Tout (see previous entry) at the top of Fore Street, or at Nicholson's Health Food Shop at the bottom (see next entry).

Situated at the bottom of Fore Street, **Nicholson's Wholefood and Health Shop** offers a wide range of health products, vitamins and herbal remedies, and a huge choice of teas as well as organic foods and environmentally friendly products. Several members of staff are trained complementary therapists, so helpful advice is on hand. It's worth scanning the notice board, which is always crammed with information about events and individuals in and around the town. Watch out for information on day-long workshops run by practising herbalists

Kingsbridge

Angela Seal and Pamela Rogers—a chance to learn how to make a poultice, an infusion or a healing creme as well as prepare nutritious meals from plants found in the fields and hedgerows. **Nicholson's Wholefood and Health Shop, 12 Fore Street ☎ 01548 854347. Open 9.00 am until 5.30 pm Monday to Saturday.**

Good Stuff

Chef Jane Twig and her partner Ben Atkinson first had the idea of providing a sandwich service from their home in Kingsbridge just over a year ago. Initially it was a question of filling a couple of baskets with freshly made sandwiches, brownies and flapjacks and taking lunch around workplaces in Kingsbridge. Now, as well as being ordered direct, Goodstuff sandwiches and salads can be picked up from local garages and village stores. Jane uses the best ingredients from local suppliers for her choice of nineteen different sandwich fillings. Most popular is chicken salad with sweet chilli mayonnaise. Brie, lettuce and cranberry relish comes a close second. Goodstuff is also developing a range of home-made meals— particularly with campers in mind, and they have just launched a fresh pizza

delivery service. With notice, Goodstuff will cater for the occasional function of up to twenty people: this could be anything from a sandwich lunch to a full blown seafood feast. They will also provide thoughtful hampers to welcome and sustain guests upon arrival at their holiday homes. **Goodstuff ☎ 01548 854662.**

Pig Finca Café

Pig Finca have a cheering knack of bringing sunshine to the dullest of days. Tucked down an alley between the opticians and the newsagents, from the outside, Pig Finca gives the impression of being a small coffee bar—this is quickly dashed on entering, as more and more rooms reveal themselves. All are splashed with hot colours and those characteristic Pig Finca touches of the 'why didn't I think of that'

variety. Daily papers are on the rack and there's a tempting—and reassuringly short—menu of fresh cooked Mediterranean food with a particular slant towards mezze and tapas dishes. Craig Franklin of Pig Finca describes the spanish wood-roasted peppers as the best in the world, and the white chocolate meringue 'Jules Jewels' is rated by my daughter Harriet as 'fab'. There is live flamenco or soft jazz on Friday evenings. Opening times: Easter–October 10.30 am–11 pm. Off-season opening times: closed Sundays and Mondays, open Tues from 6pm, rest of week open 10 am–11 pm. **Pig Finca Café ☎ 01548 855777.**

Harbour House Café

Two sisters—Gail Brendell and Scarlet Puntholer—have opened a café in Harbour House. The food is vegetarian, home-made and seasonal: on my visit in mid-November, specials included leek and potato soup, spicy vegetable casserole with naan bread, and warm apple cake with clotted cream. On warmer days, there are tables in the sunny walled courtyard garden. Open 10–5 Monday to Saturday. **Harbour House Café ☎ 01548 855666.**

Anna Graham of Good Stuff

Out from Kingsbridge

Using Kingsbridge as a base, there are many outings within easy reach: here are just three of them. Others can be found in the *Ramblers' Walks around Kingsbridge* leaflet, or the Coast and Countryside's *Salcombe–Kingsbridge Estuary Walks* booklet, which contains half a dozen new routes as well as an insight into the wildlife of the estuary.

1. Along the Estuary

A continuous walk along the estuary from Kingsbridge is hard to achieve without encountering stretches of main road. Instead, try taking a bus from the town square in Kingsbridge along the A379 towards Stokenham. The service is reasonably frequent. Frogmore and West Charleton make equally good starting points for walks, with the Charleton marshes providing opportunities for birdwatching, and Frogmore having well-marked public footpaths. There's a circular route outlined in the Kingsbridge estuary leaflet which takes in the foreshore, lime kilns, Geese Quarry and, for the final stretch, joins the green lane which was once the main route between Bowcombe and Frogmore.

If you're in Kingsbridge and you've done the shopping, the traffic's busy and you need a break, treat yourself to Walk No. 11 in the Ramblers Association's publication *Walks around Kingsbridge* [reproduced with kind permission of the South Hams Group of the Ramblers' Association]. This transports one quite dramatically from the centre of Kingsbridge to the utter quiet of Bowcombe creek. Three miles in all, the route is steep in places and sturdy footwear is advised.

2. Kingsbridge to Bowcombe circular walk (3 miles).

From Quay car park, cross the main road and take the narrow passageway by Harbour House, turning left into Ebrington Street. Go along behind the bingo hall and continue on the raised pavement towards Dodbrooke Church. Continue on up the hill, and turn right down the tarmac footpath by the phone box, past the church and between it and the vicarage. At

Bowcombe Creek

GEORGE MONTAGU

Two hundred years ago, at the top of the main street in Kingsbridge close by the boys' grammar school, there lived a very special naturalist— George Montagu. He had arrived in 1798 with his 'friend in Science' and mistress, Eliza Dorville. He was the first to describe the 'Ashy-coloured Falcon', now known as Montagu's harrier. He found it nesting on a hillside near Kingsbridge, and kept the young in one of his many aviaries until they were fully fledged. On the coast he identified the rock pipit, and was the first to describe the nesting habits of the wine-purple and slate-grey dartford warbler. But of all the birds he discovered, it is the cirl bunting that most links our time to his. He found it in 1800 at Tacket Wood, on the outskirts of Kingsbridge. Although they were known from the continent, no one had identified them in Britain before. Eliza engraved a drawing of the cirl bunting for Montagu's *Ornithological Dictionary*, which was published in 1802. Through the nineteenth and early twentieth century, cirl buntings expanded their range into Wales and northern England, but since then the range has contracted. Now there are less than 500 pairs, all in South Devon. Local farmers and the RSPB are working together to provide the grassy winter stubbles, less frequently trimmed hedges, and fields with an uncultivated fringe, which seem to favour the plant and insect species that the cirl buntings need to survive and feed their young.

Montagu shot many birds to examine them and preserve them. After his death, his collection was given to the British Museum; it even included birds he had shot during his service for Britain in the American War of Independence. He studied many other kinds of animals too: about seventy-five species of seashore creatures—shellfish, crustaceans, worms, sea-slugs and fish—were named by him, and he was the first to describe the bottle-nosed dolphin. Of all creatures he said, 'They also feel the impulse of love, the greatest dictat of nature.' In 1815 he trod on a rusty nail in his garden and contracted lockjaw. A few days after the battle of Waterloo, which had claimed three of his sons, he died.

the far end, turn left down the hill, and after a hundred yards or so turn sharply right down the valley to the farm. Continue past Washabrook Mill and then up a steep rocky lane. At the top you come to a T-junction with Buttville Hill.

Turn left, continue over the brow and descend along the track (sometimes muddy) to the road. Here you are at the head of Bowcombe Creek. Turn right along the road to Rose Cottage (note the lime kiln now used as a garage). Past the cottage, turn right up a rising footpath and continue climbing until you reach a stile. Soon after, you come into an open field. Keep straight on and walk along the lower part of the field with the hedge below on your left. Beyond the farm to the left there is a stone wall facing you; turn right up the field here to the slate stile in the top left hand corner. Cross the stile, follow the hedge and go straight forward, down the steps and into the lane. Cross over, and again go over the stile almost opposite, at the top of the steep field (Bag o' Maize Field). At the bottom of the field, cross the stile/gate into the road, and after a few paces turn left into the park, through which walk to the Embankment and on to the quay. These two routes are simple walks, but with quite a few ups and downs. The views are magnificent.

The South Hams Group of the Ramblers Association runs two or three walks a week; these average seven to nine miles. There are also shorter strolls at weekends. Non-members are welcome. A walks programme is available at Kingsbridge Tourist Information Centre. South Hams Group organiser: **Mr L. Baker ☎ 01548 580033.**

WHAT TO DO WITH SEASHORE FINDS

Quaysides and riversides can be particularly good places for finding glass pebbles and sea-worn china chips. Many interesting pieces can be found beyond slipways, and particularly around Bowcombe at low tide.

1. Put a collection of mermaid's tears (sea-smoothed glass pieces) in the bottom of a glass vase to hold flowers—or in a shallow glass dish on top of which you can put water, even floating candles.

2. String up anything with holes or a rough edge—which can be bound with a fine gauge copper wire—into a mobile. Two pieces of driftwood make good poles from which to balance your finds. String up holed limpet shells, small pieces of driftwood, even dried coloured seaweed.

3. Or try making earrings from small bunches of shells and mermaid's tears tied parcel-like with wire.

SWANS AT BOWCOMBE

At Bowcombe, walk down the lane beside the creek and you will probably see the swans. Thanks to Margaret and Peter Quick, those at Bowcombe Creek have had more success than most on the estuary. Although many swans nest by tidal estuaries, few seem to allow for the height of the tides. The high springs of mid-April, soon after the eggs have been laid, or mid-May, just before they are due to hatch, wash out many nests. The Quicks built up the nest at Bowcombe using an old pallet, and since then they have used a variety of materials to jack up the nest platform. As a result no swan has been washed out at Bowcombe for many years.

A few years ago, a pair began to construct a nest mound in the middle of the estuary, on a mud bank. As usual, the cob (the male) brought material, but it was the pen (the female) who shaped and built the nest. Several hours after she had begun, when the tide had risen and ebbed again to reveal the scarcely visible remains of the mound, the pen rebuilt it. For two weeks she continued rebuilding only to have her work destroyed by the next tide. That was an exceptionally foolish swan.

Recently, just ten days after the young had hatched, the Quicks were summoned to Collapit Creek. The Bowcombe pair had taken their family of nine the mile across the estuary, where they had found another pair with seven cygnets. The Bowcombe cob had attacked the Collapit cob, striking at him with beak and wings; he was bleeding from the head. By the time the Quicks arrived, the Collapit swans had retreated to the head of the creek, but in the confusion had been left with only three cygnets. The Bowcombe pair had sailed off with thirteen. Over the next weeks, five of the thirteen disappeared, but the remaining eight were raised successfully, as were the reduced Collapit brood. Most swans at Slapton, the River Avon and the Kingsbridge estuary have been ringed. If you see a dead swan with a coloured ring, please report the two letter code to the harbour office or Tourist Information Centre.

Bowcombe Creek Bowcombe, the northernmost finger of the estuary, is a place of bobbing boats and birdlife. Inland towards Bearscombe, the river cuts its way though picture postcard countryside, with classic farmsteads tucked between grassy meadows. Upstream from the bridge you will find a bird-viewing platform, also favoured by local artists; downstream from the bridge at the dinghy park there is a flat grassy stretch, ideal for watching the comings and goings on the water.

Bowcombe Cemetery A short walk along the main road towards Kingsbridge on the left hand side is Bowcombe Cemetery, and should it be on your mind to ponder over questions of life and death, this is the place. Obscured from both creek and roadside by a vast enclosure of trees, the cemetery is entered through weighty ironwork gates. Once inside this municipal  burial ground, it is hard to fathom what season it is, let alone the year, for it is entirely enclosed by vast evergreen oaks and Monterey pines. The rows of graves stand all the stiller between the flow of traffic on one side and water on the other. Pale blue ironwork benches that have seen better days are dotted amongst the graves.

3. Sorley Tunnel Adventure Farm

Indoor play areas, party room, pedal car track, a farm shop selling home grown vegetables and an extended school for riders. All these are new additions to the Sorley Tunnel Adventure Farm. Old favourites are still there: the turbo slides, go-karts, gladiator's course, climbing nets and death drop. Sara and Richard Balson make it their business to create diversions for children at their farm near Kingsbridge, without losing the sense of it being a working farm. Richard grows organic vegetables as part of the Riverford organic vegetable co-op. Sara runs the local vegetable box scheme. Around the farm there are lots of animals for cuddling, stroking and feeding, and should you wish to ride, Sorley has its own riding school.

See if you can walk (without a torch) all the way through the very long, blackly dark and drippy Sorley tunnel, through which steam trains once chuffed their way to Kingsbridge. The tunnel is now home to who knows what flappy, screechy creatures.

Season tickets for Sorley pay for themselves after only three visits—worth buying even for short stays.

Sorley Farm Shop and Café

Sunday lunch of home-reared organic meat and fresh picked vegetables is a steal at a fiver (£3 for children) at Sorley. And if you have room for more, there is a tempting list of substantial English puddings on the board. Sunday lunches are served between 12 and 4pm. And for those who just need something to keep them going, the cakes—cut to the size of a farm labourer's fist—are springy, wholesome and delicious. Weekday lunches might be home-made lasagne, cottage pie, or pizza; the freshly-made soup is warming and nutritious.

Richard and Sara Balsdon have made a lot of changes at Sorley. The licensed café has moved to a light new building, and **Sorley Farm Shop** is now open, where vegetables, meat , fowl, milk, pies, sausages and chutneys from the farm at Sorley and other local produce is on sale.

Loddiswell cheese is made up the road by Roger Crudge at Aveton Farm. He uses the organic cows milk from Sorley as main ingredient for the St Anton cheese, which is made in the style of a gruyère but with less salt. For a cheese with more bite, try the St Dunstone. And delicious with fresh bread and Sara Balsdon's home-made green tomato chutney is the Loddiswell goat cheese—Aveton. Heron Valley cider and juices are made a couple of miles away by Steve and Shirley Bradley at Crannacombe, or there's cider champagne from Modbury. There's stacks of organic wine and bottled beers to choose from, and for nibbles, there's Burts crisps or Tyrrells vegetable chips. Opening hours: winter 10–5, from Easter 10–6.

Directions: Coming from Kingsbridge, turn left off the B3196 just beyond Sorley Cross. There is also a regular bus service. **Sorley Tunnel Adventure Farm and Shop, Kingsbridge ☎ 01548 854078 (Riding School ☎ 01548 856662). www.sorleytunnel.com.**

MALCOLM'S GUIDE TO FISHING IN THE SOUTH HAMS

Malcolm Barnett is a local fisherman and sailor. He runs the Devon Angling Centre in Chillington.

Sea & Estuary

Strong currents sweep the coastal waters from Dartmouth to Bigbury four times a day, with the rising and falling tides. In addition, there are three estuaries draining into the coastal waters with a mixture of salt and fresh water. With all of this activity an abundance of microscopic to large sea life is drawn into the area. During the warmer months, sand eels provide the main dish for most predatory fish and are a favourite bait for many fishermen. Bass, plaice, pollack and mackerel are the fish mainly targeted by boat and shore fishermen during the summer months.

Coastal winter fishing brings a variation to the menu, with whiting, dogfish and cod, especially after dark. Charter boat fishing is available all year round, and with the skill of the skippers many large specimens can be landed from the multitude of wreck and reef sites offshore.

The estuaries themselves are also excellent for fishing, but it should be noted that all three estuaries are dedicated fish nursery areas and local restrictions and by-laws must be adhered to. During the winter months, flounders are plentiful, with many other species nearer to the seaward areas. Summer fishing brings the exclusive guilt head bream—an excellent solid flesh, and very similar to snapper served in warmer climes. For contacts in respect of charter skippers, fishing tackle, bait, day-to-day advice and tuition, **Devon Angling Centre** should be able to help.

MACKEREL FISHING KIT

Mackerel swim in large numbers close to the shore in the afternoon and early evening and are a firm favourite for family fishing. They are also delicious cooked fresh on the barbeque.

For a basic kit you will need:
Beach caster or boat rod
Reel & line, feathers and weights (cost around £40, but may be hired)
Hooks from 95p per pack
Bait from £1.70
Wellies from £12.00
Bucket £3.25

Carp & coarse

Coarse and carp fishing is a fast-growing sport, and in the South Hams we now have plenty of choice for an enjoyable day's fishing. A family favourite is Coombe Farm, situated just north of Kingsbridge, which consists of a selection of lakes with carp  and many smaller species. Bickerton Farm at North Hallsands offers a slightly more challenging rural option. Both offer day tickets at a reasonable cost. Rod licences to fish inland fresh water locations are obtainable from most Post Offices.

Fly Fishing

Seasonal salmon and sea trout fishing is available in the rivers Avon and Dart, but the rivers are strictly controlled. To obtain information on the Avon in the first instance, a good point to start is Loddiswell Post Office, which is able to issue a limited number of tickets to fish on certain stretches of the river. For fishing in the River Dart, the Sea Trout Inn at Staverton should be able to help you with up-to-date information and day tickets. If time is limited, a very favourable alternative is the large lake at Newhouse fishery near Moreleigh. Newhouse's superb lake can be as challenging as any wild lake or river to the most experienced of fishermen. Newhouse also has a well stocked beginners' lake with tackle to hire, and tuition can be arranged.

Pike Fishing

The most exciting day's pike fishing can be at Slapton Ley. This is an amazing setting and a natural Nature Reserve. The Ley is controlled by Slapton Field Centre. All fishing should be pre-booked through the centre. No fishing is allowed from the banks—only from the rowing boats provided. There are many good size pike and Eels in the Ley, all of which must be returned alive into the water. The ley at Beesands also has a stock of pike and can be fished from the bank. Fishing here is free providing you hold a rod licence.

Devon Angling Centre ☎ 01548 580888 www.devonanglingcentre.co.uk, Coombe Farm ☎ 01548 852038, Bickerton Farm ☎ 01548 511220, Newhouse Fishery ☎ 01548 821426, Slapton Field Centre ☎ 01548 580685, Loddiswell Post Office ☎ 01548 550329, Sea Trout Inn 01803 762274.

The Dart Estuary

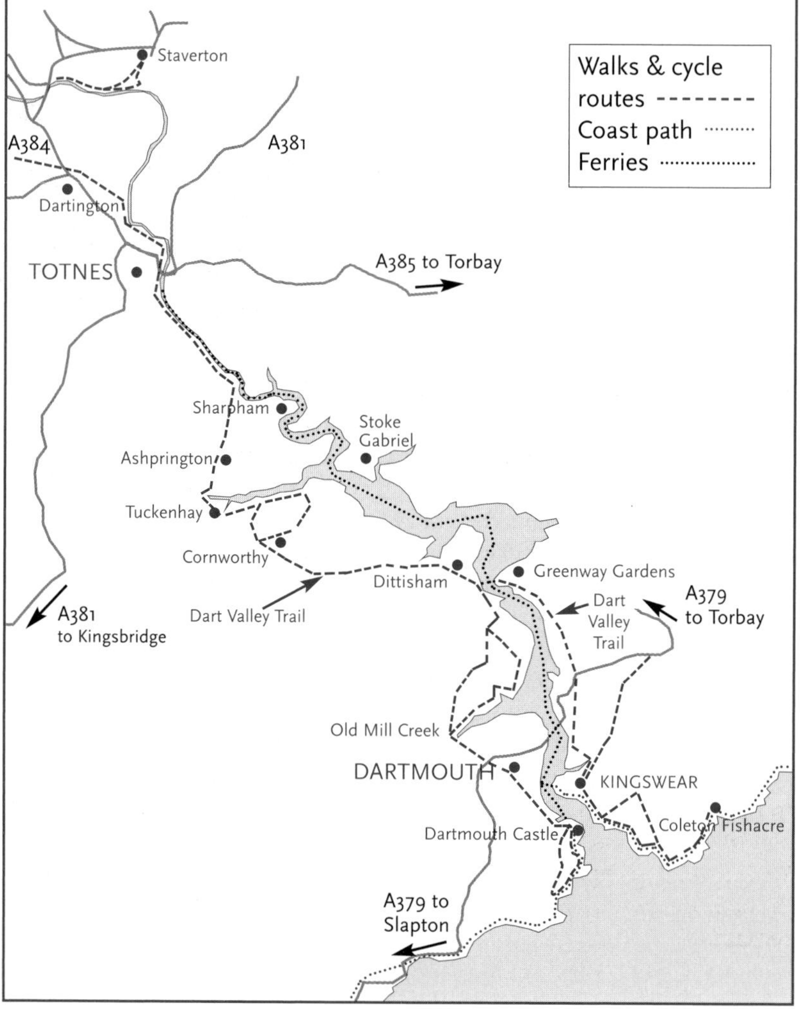

Staverton

A384

A381

Walks & cycle routes	- - - - - - -
Coast path	··········
Ferries	················

Dartington

TOTNES

A385 to Torbay

Sharpham

Stoke Gabriel

Ashprington

Tuckenhay

Cornworthy

Dittisham

Greenway Gardens

A381
to Kingsbridge

Dart Valley Trail

Dart Valley Trail

A379
to Torbay

Old Mill Creek

DARTMOUTH

KINGSWEAR

Dartmouth Castle

Coleton Fishacre

A379 to
Slapton

Chapter 3—The Dart Estuary

This chapter tackles the Dart in the direction of the incoming tide,
starting at Dartmouth and moving upstream through Dittisham,
Cornworthy and Ashprington to Totnes and Dartington.

The ria that forms the **Dart Estuary** is the longest in South Devon. A
journey down its length moves between contrasting landscapes: from
steeply wooded valleys to rolling pasture lands; from broad stretches of
deep water to the intimacy of hidden creeks, once the site of mills, which
have cut their own steep-sided and secluded valleys. Although much of
the woodland in the valley was only planted late last century, there
remain some stretches of ancient semi-natural woodland, namely the
National Trust's **Long Wood** and **Lord's Wood**. It was with oak from the
banks of the Dart that the schooners for Dartmouth's Newfoundland
fishing fleet were built. The name 'Dart' comes from the celtic word
'Darrach', which means 'oak river'. Such boatyards as remain are mainly
for the repair, refitting and storage of boats. The relative remoteness of
the villages along the west bank of the estuary, the narrow lanes leading
to them, along with the scarcity of flat land, has allowed them to escape
any major development. Being relatively frost-free, the valley used to be
known for its apple and plum orchards. Sadly, many have been lost,
though much effort is being made to conserve and replant those which
remain.

Dartmouth Castle

Dartmouth

The strong currents at the entrance to Dartmouth harbour diminish once inside the sheltered and almost completely landlocked waters at the mouth of the estuary. Daniel Defoe described Dartmouth as a port 'where five hundred sail can lie in safety'. The town's use as a haven and landing place is first recorded in Anglo-Saxon chronicles, and it was from these waters that boats departed for the Second and Third Crusades in the twelfth century. During the Middle Ages, Dartmouth established a flourishing trade with Brittany, Gascony and Spain, in wool, grain and wine.

From 1580 for around two hundred years it was the Newfoundland fisheries that bolstered Dartmouth's wealth. At its peak, hundreds of vessels left each March with a cargo of cloth, ironware and leather goods. Around a quarter of a million cod were caught in the waters off Newfoundland in a season. On shore these were gutted, dried and salted, and the oil pressed from the livers for use in the manufacture of soap and lamp oil. When the ship was full, it sailed to the Mediterranean, trading the salted

COAL LUMPERS

In the mid-19th century, gangs worked in competition with each other to refuel visiting ships. Runners were stationed at Compass point, who, when a steamer was spotted would run to tip off their gang who hung out on the embankment or Bears Cove. The first man to put his leg over the iron ladder on the wall of the cove won the right to moor the ship, and the first team to row to the ship won the contract to bunker it. These races were the forerunners of the Dartmouth Regatta's gig racing events.

fish with Catholic countries. Dried fruit and wines were brought back to England on the return journey. The houses along the Butterwalk, and other fine seventeenth-century buildings in the town, were built from the wealth brought to the town from the Newfoundland cod industry. A slump in trade in the late eighteenth century brought unemployment, poverty, over-crowding and disease. Things became only marginally better when, in the mid-nineteenth century, Dartmouth became a coaling station, fuelling visiting steamers in the Dart.

More jobs were created when the Navy established its floating training station in Dartmouth in 1863. Two wooden hulled warships, 'Britannia' and 'Hindustan', accommodated the cadets; there were also racquet courts, kennels for beagles, floating swimming baths and boat sheds at their disposal. However the overcrowded conditions on the warships prompted the building of the present Royal Naval College. Part of the Raleigh estate was compulsorily purchased, and the Edwardian College buildings, designed by Aston Webb (architect of the Victoria and Albert Museum), were completed by 1905.

Looking at the town from **Kingswear** on the opposite (eastern) bank, gives an idea how Dartmouth has developed, for all the flat ground where the shops are now was once submerged. Ray Freeman, in the publication *Devon Estuaries*, gives a picture of the changes undergone in this part of the town:

> *The Embankment which runs along the west bank of the river between the two car ferries is an example of how much of the town has been reclaimed from the mud of the river, the original bank of which was at least one*

Panorama of Dartmouth harbour

hundred yards to the west. The Boat Float entered today under the bridge on the embankment, was before 1885 open to the river, and schooners could sail up to the quay. The Royal Avenue Gardens and Coronation Park to the north are both on what was once mudflats. Under the latter lies a submarine brought in and scrapped in the 1920s and buried when the park was landscaped in the 1930s.

From the eastern bank it is also possible to see how the town was originally two separate villages—Clifton and Hardness. These fishing communities were established in the eleventh century upon the ridges either side of an inlet which ran roughly along what is now Duke's Road. Surprisingly, the process of reclamation began as early as the thirteenth century, when this inlet was dammed, creating a causeway (now Foss Street) which led to a tidal mill.

Browns Hill Steps / Dartmouth Embankment

Grapes and Gargoyles The streets of Dartmouth should be explored as they were intended: on foot or by packhorse. Eleven different flights of steps and alleyways course through this intricate and cluttered town: some of these are achingly pretty, others just plain dank. Horn's Hill and School Steps began life as conduits, taking the water from the springs in the hillside, cutting paths through the oldest parts of the town and allowing privileged views of some of the most interesting architecture. Much of it may be provincial and unsophisticated, but there are some terrific examples of local craftsmanship in all its vigour. Beasts, mermen and assorted monsters gawp from walls, pillars and doorways, around which scramble vines heaving with grapes. There's a riot of woodcarving, plasterwork, ironwork and mosaics out there. I have outlined below just some of what's on offer. A street map can be purchased from the Tourist Information Centre in Mayor's Avenue.

Woodcarving: St Saviour's Church in St Saviour's Square is one of the few buildings to survive from the fourteenth century, at which time the water lapped up to the east wall, to which ships were moored. It was over this wall that scolding wives were swung and ducked into the water at high tide. Built from wealth gathered by John Hawley from trading wine with Bordeaux, it was consecrated in 1372—although some of the fabric appears to be considerably earlier. Note the weighty door, primitively carved with lions, and the carved grapes over the altar. Guides available in the church give a detailed account of what can be seen.

The overhanging floors of **The Butterwalk** (1628–40) are also profusely carved, with quatrefoils, mermen, beasts and assorted foliage, as are the brackets. So too is the façade of 16 Clarence Hill, and in this instance the carvings are picked out in reds, blues and yellows.

The Butterwalk

Ironwork It was local foundries which produced ironwork for the town. A lovely example of its use lies in the finely proportioned **Morocco House,** one of a delightful sequence of houses along **Bayard's Cove.** Until recently, the house's ironwork was painted a playful pink and white. Up until the death of Queen Victoria, ironwork was painted in bright colours. Then it was decreed that black paint should be used as a mark of respect. And black most of it stayed.

Flock Tudor There was no shortage of work for local craftsmen when the grand houses of Fairfax Place were built in the 19th century. Their unrestrained façades imitate seventeenth century buildings as only the Victorians could, presenting riotous combinations of woodcarving and ironwork. Also note the floor mosaics—mainly black and white marble— in the occasional entrance way. These were laid by the Italian craftsmen who were shipped over with their families to make the mosaics in the Royal Naval College Chapel. These mosaics, so easily passed by unnoticed, were the results of their weekend work. A few Italian families remained in Dartmouth, going on to open the ice cream parlours and fish and chip shops in town.

Icing on the Cake There are some splendid examples of Devon lime plasterwork in Dartmouth. Following the fashion of wall painting in the 1500s, when walls were presented in surprisingly bright colours, plasterwork ceilings and overmantels became fashionable; firms of craftsmen worked exclusively in this technique, using lime plaster mixed with fine goat hair. The influence was certainly Italian, but it was the Devon craftsmen, notably the Abbot Brothers from Newton Abbot, who developed styles unique to this locality. **The Butterwalk** has particularly fine examples of this work in its first storey rooms. These merchants' houses, built in the late 1630s, once backed on to the quayside, allowing owners to keep an eye on their ships from the back window. Look round the back—there's still an iron ring for tying the boats. The wood and stone carved fronts are lovely examples of work of that time. It's worth having a coffee in the **Sloping Deck Restaurant,** above the baker's shop, if only to

Mosaic in Fairfax Place

see the fine plasterwork overmantle of the Pentecost scene.

Next door, in the room above **12 The Butterwalk**—now 'True Blue'—is a truly sumptuous plasterwork ceiling entirely covered by a Tree of Jesse. To view this, arrangements may be made to collect the key from the Guildhall ☎ **01803 832281**.

The Dartmouth Regatta

Still drawing the crowds annually at the end of August, Dartmouth Regatta first started in 1839 as a diversion for the very rich. Rowing was the focus of events, with sailing on the periphery. One hundred and sixty years on, and with a vast programme of events, the regatta draws all sorts: from the half million pound motorboat set to serious sailors, yachtsmen, rowers and scullers, to those who come just for the crack! From the moment the Mayor hands the silver oar to the Chairman of the Royal Dartmouth Regatta, until it is handed back at the closing ceremony, Dartmouth is one big picnic. Cars are banished from the streets, allowing the town to be used in the way it was intended. Dartmouth excels itself with this large scale extravaganza, making full use of the resources provided by the many military retirees and others, all of whom are used to running a tight ship.

Water Races Whaler, gig, skull, kontiki raft, dinghy, yacht—if it floats, it races in regatta week. Local rowing events are hugely popular. The regatta has seven whalers and seven blue boats which are brought out of store for local teams to practise. Friday is local rowing day: competition is ferocious, in particular the licensed victuallers' men's whaler race. Come the evening, with races won and lost, the pubs are exceptionally lively.

Between the abseiling wall and the tennis courts is the **Craft Tent**, a perfect opportunity to check out some of the best local produce and crafts without rushing about the countryside.

Red Arrows For many it's a family ritual that ranks as high as harvest festival or the County Show. There's a great feeling of holiday. Hours before the display (usually held on the first Saturday of the

Dartmouth from Dyer's Hill

regatta), families spill on to Dyer's Hill above the estuary. Picnics are produced, and everyone settles in for a good evening. Burgers and hot dogs are laid on for the less organised. At exactly six-thirty, a tiny glistening dot emerges from the far reaches of the Dart. Seconds later, flying in exact formation,

the Red Arrows tear down the estuary, blasting trails of coloured smoke behind them. The Red Arrows have been appearing at the Regatta since the late seventies. It's a 'high' or 'low' show, depending on cloud cover. The display lasts around twenty-five minutes. The cliffs, coastline, estuary and steep-sided valleys provide a stunning setting for the Arrows: the focus is drawn in as they skim the water, and then out as they burst skyward with stomach-pulling verticals, which burst into cascades of colour over the fields and water below. Afterwards, there's a couple of hours to spend at the fair before dark, when the firework display begins.

Regatta Fireworks Getting a deck chair around the boat float on fireworks night is a bit like getting a ticket for the Wimbledon Final. It's not a question of camping overnight, but certainly over tea. Families arrive around 4 pm, a good five hours before lighting the touch paper. Firework displays are on Thursday and Saturday nights at around 9 pm—check the programme for details. **www.dartmouthregatta.co.uk.**

Dartmouth Film Society

Conceived in 1997 over a cup of coffee, the Dartmouth Film Society continues to thrive. It provides its members with a full and varied programme throughout the year. The society meet in the Guildhall once a fortnight not the most comfortable of venues, but there is a bar and chocolates and quite a party atmosphere. Showings are very well attended, and no longer punctuated by jeers when the projector breaks down, as the society has been awarded funding to buy a new one. The programme is devised to appeal to all tastes, embracing foreign language, mainstream and independent films. A membership fee of £22.00 a year covers all showings apart from the special outdoor evenings. For 2005, a Bollywood musical is planned under the stars at Bayards Cove to coincide with the music festival in May. Temporary members welcome. **Dartmouth Film Society ☎ 01803 835849.**

Dartmouth Food Festival

Since Tom Jaine and Joyce Molyneaux opened the Carved Angel in 1974, Dartmouth has been associated with outstanding food. Cooks who learned their craft at the Carved Angel moved on to open their own restaurants, while more culinary talent blew in to the mouth of the Dart from the cities. With so much knowledge upon the doorstep, it seemed sensible to make use of it, and in October 2004 the first Dartmouth Food Festival was launched. For three days the town became almost edible with restaurants and bars hosting all manner of feasts, tastings, samplings and soirées, while the market place was hijacked for cooking demonstrations, workshops and a farmers market. Festival organiser Paul Allen is already stuck into the planning of the next, even bigger festival, so please come with an appetite to match. Ask at the Tourist Information Centre for details of the programme.

The Flavel Centre

This much needed community centre, bang in the middle of Dartmouth, has been built upon the site of the old fire station and Flavel Church Hall. The elegant £2 million building is the fruit of eight years' hard work by various committees, supporters and volunteers.

The project has been a strenuous community effort. Local people were involved in the fundraising, the choice of architect (which was decided by public vote) and even the nature of the building itself.

From the outside, the contemporary glass and concrete structure sits easily amongst the traditional tall Dartmouth buildings with steep pitched roofs which surround it. Delabole slate reused from the old fire station faces the front wall of the building giving it a mellow and comfortable quality. Inside, The welcoming oak reception desk crafted by local furniture maker Nick Carey is attended by one of the centre's many volunteer helpers. On the ground floor is **Flavours Café**, which overlooks Avenue Gardens, and the spacious library with IT suite, occupies the rest of the ground floor. Upstairs is the main auditorium which is used for cinema screenings three times a week, including 'The Big Scream', an exclusive lunchtime screening for parents and carers with their babies of up to twelve months old, and the price includes coffee and bus pick up and drop home! There is also a gallery space, a small studio and a green room. The place teems with activities of all kinds, the library is filled with hush, and the café roars. **The Flavel Centre and Flavours Café ☎ 01803 839530. www.theflavel.org.uk.**

Dartmouth

As autumn sets in, Dartmouth boats are put into store, and the crowds start to thin. Out of season the pace is less frantic, and shopkeepers can give their customers more time and attention. Specialising as it does in the 'not immediately necessary' things of life, Dartmouth is a brilliant place for seeking out unusual gifts.

Books
The Harbour Bookshop (formerly owned by *the* Christopher Robin, son of A.A. Milne) will not only advise on books, but they will also order, gift wrap and mail a book of your (or their) choice complete with card. Beat that, amazon.co.uk!

For those who love secondhand books, the **Church of St Barnabus** on Newcomen Road is stuffed with yards of them from floor to ceiling. **Harbour Bookshop, 12 Fairfax Place** ☎ 01803 832448.

Flowers & Food
The Smith Street Delicatessen Partners Marcelle Chownes-Dove and Simon Entwhistle have combined their respective passions—flowers and food—in this small shop in Smith Street. An uncommon and inspiring collection of both: Birds of Paradise,

Parrot Tulip, Wax Flower and shamrock were some of the flowers on the chalkboard on the day of my visit. I also noticed pretty baskets of grape hyacinths for the more enduring purchase. Marcelle orders direct from Holland, and the flowers are delivered chilled every Tuesday afternoon. For the quality of flower, the price is reasonable, and no matter how small your purchase, it is wrapped beautifully in contrasting tissue paper and bound with raffia.

The food is just as inspiring. Great strings of capsicums and chillies hang from the ceiling, and the shelves are stacked with the exotic and unfamiliar. Watch out for the colourfully decorated boxes of rough sugar pieces, the Brownes chocolates (made in Throwleigh), Lavinia's Larder Rhubarb and Raspberry Jam (made in Halwell). On top of the chiller there are olives to taste (try the lime vega).

If you're stuck for a present idea, Smith Street Hampers are enormously popular. They are skillfully assembled by Simon to suit the budget of the giver and the needs of the receiver. **Smith Street Delicatessen, The Old Shambles, Smith Street** ☎ 01803 835900.

Clothes
And if you can't face shopping for clothes in big stores, Dartmouth is packed with small clothes shops, with lots of good names scattered amongst the rails of the small and friendly stores. **White Stuff** in Victoria Road has some wonderfully unrestrained shirts, fluffy fleeces, and rangy sports gear. **Riverside Fashions**, on the other hand, make it their business to keep their customers warm. dry and comfortable, and **True Blue** in the Butterwalk has clobber that's nautical but nice. **White Stuff, 11 Victoria Road** ☎ 01803 834006. **Riverside Fashions, Fairfax Place** ☎ 01803 832125. **True Blue, 12 Duke Street** ☎ 01803 835556.

Hairdressing
The Cutting Lounge For a pampering haircut this small salon in Lower Street is the place. Chris Watson, Laura Hannaford and their team not only deliver dreamy head massages, use deliciously gentle products and ply you with steaming coffee, but they also do a terrific cut, while you catch up on the latest issue of *Hello* magazine. **The Cutting Lounge, 37a Lower Street** ☎ 01803 839660

Dartmouth

Liquor

Dartmouth Vintners

With a history of trading wine with Bordeaux and port with Oporto, it follows that there should be an excellent vintners in Dartmouth. There is an extensive range of wines, spirits and beers in this shop on the corner of The Butterwalk. Wines here are nearly all from small independent producers. Staff at Dartmouth Vintners enjoy discussing needs with their customers, from the 'under a fiver' wine for the Sunday roast, to the finer details of malt whiskies, over eighty of which form part of a vast collection of miniatures. Local brews are also well supported, with Sharpham wines, Crannacombe cider, Bramley and Gage liqueurs and Blackawton beer being just some of the South Hams produce on sale. Watch out for the Quinta da Eira Velha—a vintage port from a Portuguese quinta owned by the Newman family, who own and still live at Blackpool Sands. There's an original bottle of Newman's port exhibited upstairs in the museum. And if you're looking for a good Bordeaux, try the red Le Voyageur 1994. **Dartmouth Vintners, 6 Duke Street ☎ 01803 832602.**

Bags & buckets:

The Canvas Factory

Doug Briscoe, from Georgia USA, chartered his 60-foot yacht for some years, firstly around the Caribbean and later from Dartmouth. On board he had a sewing machine, which he used to repair sails and awnings. After circumnavigating the globe in 1994–95 he sold the

boat, but kept the sewing machine. Those were the beginnings of The Canvas Factory, which he opened in Foss Street in July 1996. Using 15–18 oz Indian canvas, Doug Briscoe constructs containers of all shapes and sizes, working from traditional patterns: the classic American ice bag, for example, forms the basis of The Canvas Factory shopping bag; and a horse's nose bag is the inspiration behind (surprise!) their Nose Bag. From the pencil cases, spectacle bags, and baby buckets, to vast grip bags, cruising bags and laundry buckets. The Canvas Factory manages to make things which are absolutely functional as well as being wonderful objects in their own right. Goods are available by mail order, or (costing a little less) at **The Canvas Factory, 5 Foss Street ☎ 01803 832186.**

Art and Crafts in Dartmouth

There's a vibrant art scene in Dartmouth. Watch out for the Galleries Festival which takes place around the end of May and provides an annual focus for the artist's community here. Below is a selection of just a few galleries which are well worth a visit.

Hartworks shows the work of Simon Hart and other artists from the South-west. **Hartworks, ☎ 01803 839000. www.hartworks.co.uk**

Andras Kaldor Gallery shows intricate architectural paintings all done without the help of a ruler. **Andras Kaldor Gallery, 15 Newcomen Road ☎ 01803 833874.**

Coombe Gallery opened in 2004, with an emphasis on contemporary figurative and abstract work by leading painters and applied artists. **Coombe Gallery 20 Foss Street ☎ 01803 835820. www.coombegallery.com**

Doug Briscoe of The Canvas Factory

Dartmouth

Imago exhibit a diverse range of contemporary jewellery, both precious and non-precious, by both leading makers and promising newcomers. **Imago, 22 Fairfax Place ☎ 01803 835105.**

Simon Drew Gallery Drew's witty pen and ink drawings have found their way onto mugs, teeshirts and aprons in this entertaining gallery in Foss Street. **Simon Drew Gallery, 13 Foss St ☎ 01803 833534.**

Higher Street Gallery This Crafts Council selected gallery, housed in the fifteenth-century Merchants House, is a mixed arts and crafts gallery and shows the work from the best of British makers—over a hundred of them. **Higher Street Gallery, 1 Higher Street ☎ 01803 833157.**

The D'Art Gallery exhibits a discerning selection of contemporary

art from UK artists together with affordable prints. **D'Art Gallery, 4 Lower Street ☎ 01803 834923. www.dart-gallery.com**

The Stewart Gallery provides the opportunity to visit the artists studio. James Stewart's colourful work is wide ranging in subject and style. **The Stewart Gallery, 3 Market Place ☎ 01803 839555. www.stewartgallery.co.uk**

Food

Dartmouth has become a centre for good eating. Here are just a few places of quality.

The Crab Shell is a tiny kiosk tucked away in Raleigh Street (known locally as 'Raleigh Slip' since it was originally a slipway to the river), which runs between Newcomen Road and Lower Street. It serves seafood sandwiches to take away (or if you prefer you can just buy the seafood). There is one choice of bread (hooray, no decisions to make)— the freshest of light wholemeal, generously filled with one of seven options. Local crab is a speciality, or smoked or kiln roast salmon from Dartmouth Smokehouse. Sandwiches are simply presented and packaged. No frisée lettuce or other such fripperies. A terrific formula. Knockout

sandwiches at reasonable prices. **Crab Shell Seafood and Sandwich Bar, Raleigh Street ☎ 01803 839036. Open March–November 10.30 am–2 pm.**

The Singing Kettle This small café serves a good home-made junket, amongst a menu of scrumptious boy's favourite school puddings. Cook Debbie Morris makes these enduring puddings as well as fresh springy and delicious cakes. The Devon apple cake and carrot cake disappear very rapidly, I'm told. Tucked away from the main drag, The Singing Kettle attracts local custom, and keeps prices down. **The Singing Kettle, 6 Smith Street ☎ 01803 832624. Open Tuesday to Sunday 10–5.**

For those who missed breakfast or just want another one, it has to be a

Dartmouth

trip to **Alf Resco's**. This busy café hangs loose. Here families can eat and drink together, or sit around reading newspapers and drinking coffee. Alf Resco's extended breakfasts are served from 7 am–2 pm, Wednesday through Sunday. Try scrambled eggs with smoked salmon, or baguettes packed with salami or mozzarella and tomato. And as the name suggests, there is a vine-shaded terrace with a flaming torch over the archway where we can pretend the sun shines. **Café Alf Resco, Lower Street ☎ 01803 835880.**

The Anzac Street Bistro
Sarin Aubry, Alison Aubrey and Shonagh Simmonds met up when working at Conran's 'Le Pont de La Tour' restaurant on the South Bank. The food is fresh and seasonal, with many of the ingredients produced at the family farm in Blackawton. Chef Shonagh Simmonds describes the influence as being 'slightly French'. See for yourselves. A meal is very fairly priced. given the quality of the food and credentials of the chefs, and a bottle of house wine is £9.00.
The Anzac Street Bistro, 2 Anzac Street ☎ 01803 835515.

Two Hotels
An inn since 1736, and host to numerous distinguished guests, including the original Siamese twins, Chang and Eng, who lived joined at the hip till they were sixty-four, it would be easy to dwell upon the heritage of such a venerable institution as the **Royal Castle Hotel**. The present owner, Nigel Way, however, looks to the future. What at first sight seems a busy but fairly traditionally run hotel, is nothing of the sort. For Mr Way and his staff have put into action the greenest of working practices. Low energy light bulbs, refillable jars, and jugs of milk (no nasty cartons), bicycles for hire, recycling and buying locally are all the order of the day. When guests arrive at the Royal Castle, their cars are valet parked—a polite way of saying that they are taken away from them. Mr Way then seizes his moment and presents the (now carless) visitor with a pamphlet of suggestions of places to go and things to do without a car in and around Dartmouth. From a self-guided walk about town to more ambitious itineraries of 'boat there, train back' trips to Totnes. Excuses like 'I haven't got a bicycle' hold about as much water as his low-

flush loos. The hotel is happy to provide these— bicycles, that is—along with backpacks and packed lunches. **Royal Castle Hotel, The Quay ☎ 01803 833033.**
Browns Hotel This small townhouse hotel in Victoria Road has recently been transformed into a sleek and contemporary place to stay. Fun touches give rooms individuality (some with leather curtains or funky fabrics on the chairs)—all have big duvets, feather pillows, Roberts radios and fresh coffee. A leisurely breakfast of home-made and locally produced food may be taken at wooden tables, with plenty of room to read the paper. In the evenings, freshly made tapas dishes are served in Browns Bar, where the comfortable sofas soon fill up with locals tempted by the spiced nuts, stuffed grilled mussels, tuna cakes with spicy relish, spicy chorizo, smoked mushrooms and other delicacies.
Browns Hotel, 27–29 Victoria Street ☎ 01803 832572 www.brownshotel dartmouth.co.uk

Out and About in Dartmouth

There are plenty of ways of getting out onto the water, and here are some of them . . .

On the Water

Take your time to mosey up and down the river. Self-drive boats are available for half and full days from the Dartmouth Boat Hire Centre. **Dartmouth Boat Hire Centre** ☎ **01803 722367.**

Riverlink For a comfortable trip to Totnes and back Riverlink provides a reliable service—watch out for special themed trips. Boats depart from the Steamer Quay on the east bank close to the Riverlink office. **Riverlink** ☎ **01803 834488 www.riverlink.co.uk.**

Boat Charter Seeing the coastline from the the sea puts a whole new perspective on a familiar place. Owner and skipper Tony Hoile offers trips on his boat 'Falcon' around the South Devon coast and up the River Dart. 'Falcon'—a twin engine Fairey Bulldog—can be charted for anything from two hours up to a whole day, and is licensed to carry 12 passengers. Tony shares his detailed knowledge of the wildlife in the area, and takes his passengers to tucked-away coves and secluded inlets, where he might turn off the engine, drop anchor and watch the comings and goings while the kettle boils (tea and biscuits are provided). There may be sightings of, amongst others, peregrines, seals, fulmars, terns and kestrels. With thirty years of experience of diving this area, Tony is full of fascinating stories and information about the coast. ☎ **01803 839245** ☎ **07970 759172 www.DartBoat.com.**

Dartmouth to Dittisham 'Champion Sturdy' and 'Warrior' are David Ridalls' classic wooden launches which ferry passengers between Dartmouth and Dittisham. The service runs at least hourly between March and the end of October, and half hourly in the high season. Boats leave

On the ferry to Kingswear / Dartmouth Passenger Ferry

BEGINNER'S GUIDE TO SCUBA DIVING AND SNORKELLING IN THE SOUTH HAMS

Tony Hoile (see facing page) is a local diving instructor with 30 years experience. Co-founder of Totnes Sub-Aqua Club, he has an extensive knowledge of diving in the area and now runs a diving charter boat.

Learn to dive with a qualified and recognised diving school (either the British Sub-Aqua club, or PADI, or through a local BSAC). There is a thriving club in Totnes that provides training and organises dives around the coast. To find out more visit **www.totnes-bsac.co.uk.**

BASIC SNORKELLING KIT

Mask – tempered glass face plate, nose piece and adjustable strap.

Snorkel – use a clear snorkel (without a valve).

Fins (flippers) – make sure the blade is rigid. Slipper-type fins are more comfortable.

Wet suit – not essential, but keeps you warmer.

With some training under your belt, it is best to start out with shallow shore dives before progressing to the deeper waters. The coast of the South Hams holds some superb shallow shore dives for scuba divers. Access is not always easy, but shore dives may be made from Blackpool Sands (either side of the beach near the rocks), Torcross (below the cliffs), Beesands (at the northern end of the beach road), Hallsands (either below the old hotel or to the north of the beach under Tinsey Head), Hope Cove (use the slipway immediately below the car park), and Thurlestone (the reefs below the sandy beach have lots of life, and the wreck of the 'Louis Shields' lies here).

Much of the marine life lies in shallow water under brown kelp that grows in the summer. There are many types of anemones to be seen, and territorial fish such as wrasse and blennies. During the spring and early summer cuttlefish and john dory are often to be seen.

Take care on entry and exit, as the rocks are slippery and uneven. Plan where you are going to exit, and beware of the tidal stream as it can be swift. Use a surface marker buoy to indicate your presence to other water users. Do not dive in harbour entrances and channels.

Snorkelling around the shallow water at rocks' edge is an easier way of viewing underwater life. All the sites mentioned above are equally good for snorkelling. Stay in close and you will be amazed at the amount of marine life at the water's edge. Make sure the conditions are calm. Local swimming pools now conduct basic instruction for snorkelling for adults and children. For more information visit the British Sub-Aqua Club website: **www.bsac.org.uk.**

from the North Embankment, by Avenue Gardens, and a return trip for adults is £5.00 (children £3.00). A peaceful trip with conversation rather than commentary, on beautiful old boats (which are also available for private charter). **David Ridalls ☎ 07818 001108. For ferry times: www.dittisham.org.uk.**

The Picnic Boat The picnic boat can be chartered for winding up the Dart, eating fine foods and sipping champagne. Liz Macarthur offers all kinds of trips along the river: a romantic trip for two with luxury hamper and champagne; a family day out with a spot of fishing; a river pub tour; and for those who like to dress up, a pirate picnic. **Liz MacArthur ☎ 07968 785650 www.thepicnicboat.co.uk.**

Canoe Adventures This friendly company offers the opportunity to explore the Dart and Salcombe estuary aboard a lone Voyager 12-seat canoe. Each canoe comes with steersman, skills, buoyancy aids, paddles, picnic blankets, eco-friendly barbeque, tea, coffee and hot chocolate. Aside from a straightforward daytime paddle, Phil Sheardown and his team put on special moonlight trips with a pub supper, picnic paddles, campfire storytelling, bushcraft days, and wild food outings. Canoe adventures can also provide 2-seat canoe training and guided whitewater in winter. In early Spring, Voyager races are held alongside The Maltsters Arms on Bow Creek at Tuckenhay, for the RNLI and the Chernobyl Childrens' Project; you can take part in the furious paddling, or just watch from the shore, drink in hand. Call for details and date. The company is currently developing a lateen and leeboard sailing rig for the canoes, and an eco-friendly campfire brazier for the outdoors market. Prices range from £17 per seat per tide, to £158 per tide for the whole canoe. **☎ 01803 865301 www.canoeadventures.co.uk.**

On Dry Land

The Walks The first of these is to Old Mill Creek, the first creek upstream from Dartmouth. The walk takes in the church at Townstal, and descends into the quiet of this lovely creek, where many of the Dartmouth boats are repaired. Warfleet is the second outing: this takes in Dartmouth Castle. Then it's over the river to Kingswear by ferry for the third outing, a fairly strenuous walk which goes as far as the National Trust gardens of Coleton Fishacre. There is an option to return to Kingswear along the coast path, and there is a trip to Stoke Gabriel on the east bank of the Dart, travelling by boat from Dartmouth. Finally, there's an option to walk into town from Little Dartmouth.

Walk 1: Old Mill Creek

A short way upriver from Dartmouth on the west bank is Old Mill Creek. As it is not possible at the time of writing to take a flat route along the water's edge from the town, because of restricted MoD property, we follow part of the Dart Valley Trail up to Townstal. To get there, at the end of Foss Street turn left up Browns Hill Steps. From Browns Hill, turn left uphill along Clarence Hill. Cross Victoria Road and walk up Church Road to Townstal Church.

The church is the oldest in Dartmouth, and is approached by a yew-studded pathway through the graveyard. Over the years, movement in the ground has shifted the stones into a disorderly gathering, studded with angels, chains and anchors.

From the church, cross the main road (College Way) into Old Mill Road. This steeply winding road leads down to the head of Old Mill Creek. A single house, and boat sheds for maintenance and repair, are the only buildings in the creek. At low tide it is empty of boats save for a few discarded vessels. The foreshore is busy with gulls, herons and redshanks feeding in the mud. In the summer, common and arctic terns can be seen here, and occasionally black terns visit. From here it is possible to follow a permissive path along the northern shore which is close to the water's edge, or continue the walk along the public footpath to Dittisham as outlined in the Dart Valley Trail (leaflets are on sale at Dartmouth Tourist Information Centre).

From the Water A visit by water is recommended: Old Mill Creek is accessible for one and a half hours either side of high tide. On the southern side of the bank on the foreshore at Sandquay Woods is Hermitage Castle. This extraordinary structure is built into the steep bank beside the water's edge. Entered from a grassy clearing in the woods above, steps

Old Mill Creek / A mariner's grave in Townstal churchyard

descend into deepening dark-
ness, finally arriving at shore
level. Sadly, the building is in
such disrepair that it is now
unsafe to enter. It was probably
built around 1800, when ladies
passed the time there sewing
stumpwork or painting watercolours, even taking a dip in the
waters from the earthy bathing
house below. The castle is just
one of many remnants of the
Raleigh Estate, upon which the
Royal Naval College is now built.

SOCKS THAT STARTLE

Several years ago, little egrets were a
rare sight on the estuary. Now these
smaller all-white versions of herons,
more usually found in France and
further south, have made their home
here. Their bright yellow legs give a clue
to their strange method of fishing:
waving their legs around in the shallows to startle the fish, which
momentarily stop in their tracks, giving
the little egret the opportunity to seize
the fish with his beak.

A pleasure garden, and a
grotto fashioned from moss lichen and tree stumps, which may well have
supported its own resident hermit, were also part of what was known as
Mount Boone. In the mud at Hermitage Creek lie the bulky remains of
an old Colchester barge, with grass growing from its hull like cress in an
eggshell. Further out in the creek on a mudbank is the wreck of the Irish
sailing coaster 'Invermore' of Castleford. The wreck of the Spanish
galleon 'Madre de Dios' is also thought to be somewhere in the creek.
After it was captured from the tail end of the Armada fleet, the ship had
been brought into Dartmouth and used as a hospital ship, most probably
in Old Mill Creek. A whale was washed up in Old Mill Creek in 1865, and
more recently a school of confused porpoises became marooned in its
waters. More contemporary itinerants found their way to the Creek in the
eighties, when a group of Irish houseboat dwellers moored up there for
a spell. It is a romantic and intriguing place.

Walk 2: Warfleet

Easily overlooked, Warfleet is a quiet creekside community tucked
beneath the road which leads to the Dartmouth Pottery. Sketched by the
painter J.M.W. Turner on a visit to Devon in 1811, this quiet inlet remains
a community apart. It has escaped prettying up and labelling, and long
may it remain thus. An elderly resident swims daily in the creek, on the
shores of which are lime kilns. Close by is the Boat House, which stands
on the pebble beach, available for holiday lets. This has the sure sniff of
adventure. Warfleet is easily walked to from town via the Newcomen

GURGLY JUG

A dubious connection with the Newfoundland cod trade is the 'gurgel krug', 'pichet glou glou' or 'jarro gorgoteante', sold widely as a souvenir in the 1960s and 1970s. It's a jug in the body of a curled-tailed cod, which, when water is poured through its gaping mouth, produces deep gurgly sounds. Margaret Thatcher, when presented with one in 1978, thought it would go 'very well with the decorations at Downing Street'.

Road. At the viaduct, take the path which leads down to Warfleet.

Further up the road is what was until recently the **Dartmouth Pottery**, a rare example of industrial architecture in Dartmouth. Mills have been in existence on this site since the mid-seventeenth century. The pottery building used to be a paper mill. Over the main entrance across the footbridge are the letters 'A.H.H.', the initials of Dartmouth entrepreneur and landowner Arthur H. Holdsworth. The Mill, once powered by a mammoth water-wheel fifty feet in diameter, produced a high quality paper from coloured cotton rags. The paper was used, amongst other things, for the local Dartmouth banknotes: a £1 note survives in the town museum. Subsequently, the mills produced flour and, after the wheel had been used for firewood, it became a brewery, producing first 'Barley Wine from the English Rhine', then 'Warfleet Pale Ales—the finest beer in Britain', using the pure water from the valley stream for washing bottles and for the beer itself. Mud from the mill pond fed the market garden alongside it, which grew soft fruits and vegetables, and later watercress. After years of lying empty, commandos used the building as their headquarters during World War II, and in 1948 it became a pottery.

In the 1950s and 1960s Dartmouth Pottery produced 'Polka Dot' ware, 'Cottage' ware and the hugely popular 'Motto' ware. Collectors of pottery are advised to scour the local charity shops and jumble sales for it.

Then in the 90s there was the exuberant Rainbow Ware of

WARFLEET KILNS

In the nineteenth century, itinerants and local children were attracted by the warmth of a working lime kiln. The unfortunate Henry Avis, aged 12, was burnt to death at the Warfleet kilns when he accidentally fell asleep and rolled into the burning kiln. By all accounts he was a lonely boy, who lived with his grandfather at the public baths near the castle.

Marjya Boxer: in the shape of hearts, petals, diamonds and squares, in a range of strong colours. Sadly missed by many kitchens.

The Castle

From Warfleet you can wander along the road, which will take you to Dartmouth Castle. Alternatively, a small passenger ferry chugs between Bayard's Cove and the Castle.

Boat rides for small children can be an adventure—for about five minutes. An ideal trip for those with little ones is to the castle from the town. The experience of being in a small boat and seeing Dartmouth from the water, albeit briefly, is a delightful and inexpensive one. At the castle end there are a lot of steps to climb, but once at the top the excuse to pause is the church of **St Petrox**—spare and bleak in its simplicity, and exposed to the brunt of the weather. The earliest record of a place of worship on this site predates the Norman conquest. It's a sobering place, suited to reflection and prayer. Should you wish to attend a service, evensong is nightly at 6.30.

Dartmouth Castle Hewn from—and into—the rock face at the mouth of the estuary, the castle is just one of four defences built on the site to protect Dartmouth from attackers. Building started in 1481 by order of Edward IV, and the castle was completed by 1494. The first in the country to be designed for artillery, guns were placed in the basement near the waterline, while the soldiers were accommodated in the floors above. At times of threat, a chain was stretched across the water to Gomerock, close to Kingswear Castle which stands on the opposite bank. Now and then, vivid re-enactments are staged around the defences: groups set up camp, living, working, fighting, eating and dressing in fifteenth-century style. The Castle is a tremendous setting for such an event, and young audiences love it. **Dartmouth Castle ☎ 01803 833588.**

Coastward from the Castle Dartmouth Castle is worth noting for its woodland and coast walks alone. An information board in the castle car park shows four easy waymarked trails to follow. These include walks to Gallants Bower, where earth banks are all that remain of a royalist fort; and a walk to Sugary Cove, with steps leading down to the beach. A walk to the Coastguard's Cottages along the springy grass and heathland is strewn with sea kale in the early summer, and an excellent source of sloe berries in the autumn.

Notes on the coast

Castle Cove was once lined with coloured beach huts and diving boards. Traditionally it was a place where Dartmouth children learned to swim. The public baths were also nearby. A little further round the coast is Ladies Cove which, as its name suggests, was reserved for ladies' swimming only. Each season, bathing machines were floated round to the cove, where they were used for transporting delicate Victorian ladies into the restorative waters without risking an unseemly exposure of flesh.

Compass Point: A lookout point since the year dot: in the early 1600s, a compass and watch house were built here, 'to discern and try the winds and keep the sea watch as in ancient time hath been accustomed'.

Warren Point: Rabbits were a thirteenth-century introduction to Britain from Italy. Rabbit husbanders didn't know the half of it when they set about the practice of commercial rabbit breeding. A commercial rabbit warren was registered here at Warren Point in 1613. Rabbits were bred for their meat and fur; they were kept in pillow mounds, and granite vermin traps were set for unfortunate predators.

Walk 3: Bramble Jelly and Beyond

A coastal walk from Kingswear to Coleton Fishacre. A pound for the ferry and a couple more for preserves should cover the cost of this trip discovering the coastal area around Kingswear.

Take the Lower Ferry from near Bayard's Cove to Kingswear. First follow the coast path 'acorn' sign, then take the route under the archway opposite The Royal Dart Hotel, and climb up Alma Steps. Note the small garden reserved for the use of the elderly of the parish. Once on Beacon Road, houses, plants and vistas begin to grow larger. Here in late summer Agapanthus grow to massive proportions amongst the generous fans and spires of other subtropical plants.

On the seaward side of the road, astonishingly steep gardens descend the cliffs, obscuring views of the estuary mouth below. Close by, at the water's edge, is Kingswear Castle, the location of which is so exposed to salt and water that the original iron guns corroded and had to be replaced with brass ones. The Castle itself is available for rent through the Landmark Trust—for that elemental break! On the hill above is another fortification, Fort Ridley, which last saw action during the Civil War.

Veering a little away from the coast, the lane becomes short and steep and barely wide enough for one person. Rocky Lane follows the line of a spring. It is here that jars of home-made preserves may be on sale.

AUTUMN HEDGE TREATS

When walking in the autumn, remember to take a bag to fill with berries and nuts. Early autumn treats will include the obvious blackberries—and the less picked elderberries (delicious stewed with apples or turned into wild Ribena—see below). Later in the season, green hazelnuts are delicious from their shells, ripe rosehips, rowans and haws from prickly hawthorn bushes, and sloes as already mentioned earlier. Leave some berries to see the birds through the colder months. Try making jam or cordial to enjoy in deepest winter.

HEDGEROW JELLY

Pick a quantity of each of the following: elderberries, rosehips, blackberries, sloes and crab apples. Exact proportions are not that important—but don't let one dominate or it will mask the other flavours. Rinse the fruits well and chop the crab apples. Put into a large pan with a base covering of water. Cook well until soft, then mash with a potato masher to form a thick pulp. Strain the pulp through a jelly bag or muslin tied to the legs of an upturned stool. Leave overnight to drip. Measure the resulting juice. Put in a large pan with 1 lb white granulated sugar to every pint of juice. Stir until the sugar has dissolved then boil rapidly until set point has been reached (104 degrees on a jam thermometer—or put a little on a cold saucer in the fridge and see if a skin forms on it). Put into warm sterilised jars (under a low grill or 2 minutes in microwave for 6 jars), cover when still hot and label. NB: consider where you pick your fruits—'wild' does not equal 'organic'.

ELDERBERRY CORDIAL

Strip berries off the stems and place in a large pan (stainless steel if possible) with a little water to simmer. When the berries are reduced to a juice, strain the resulting purple liquid and add 8 ounces of white sugar to each pint of juice. Simmer again for a few minutes to dissolve (but not to cook like jam). Pour into clean glass bottles with screw top lids. The cordial will keep for months in a cool dark place. It is full of vitamin C. Dilute with hot or cold water as with Ribena.

BLACKBERRY JAM

Remove stalks, wash and drain fruit. Crush the fruit and bring slowly to the boil, stirring continuously. Add 3/4 lb sugar to each pound of fruit and boil till set; 30–40 minutes. Pour into clean dry jars and seal.

Depending on season, it may be bramble jelly, a more exotic peach or plum preserve, marmalade, even fruit butters such as organic Lemon Butter with Elderflower. Look out for an 'eggs for sale' note pinned to the gate behind the table, for they are very special big chocolatey brown speckled Maran eggs.

Carry on up the lane, past Brownstone car park on the right and on to **Coleton Fishacre**, the landscaped gardens and house of the D'Oyly Carte family—of Sadler's Wells and Gilbert and Sullivan fame. To enjoy this National Trust property to the full, you will need plenty of reserves of energy, for this plantsman's garden, developed over the years between 1926–47 by Rupert and Dorothy D'Oyly Carte, covers acres of steeply wooded ground and supports a wide range of tender and uncommon trees. It is perhaps at its best in springtime, when the camellias, rhododendrons and magnolias are in full force. A reviver in the pretty tea garden is recommended before setting out on the return journey. A military road leads past the limestone day beacon, which has served as a navigational point for boats since the 1870s. There follows a muscle-toning stretch as the coast path is rejoined for the last leg back to the village of Kingswear. **Coleton Fishacre, Brownstone, Kingswear ☎ 01803 752466.**

Walk 4: Stoke Gabriel

Mosey upriver to Stoke Gabriel from Dartmouth. This pretty village is clustered around a millpool, and only separated from the Dart by a dam wall. Disembark at the pontoon, walk across the causeway (taking care not to trip over crabbers) and around the edge of the millpond (at high tide, take the road up to the village). Beside the Church is Church Orchard, one of the few remaining ancient apple orchards in the South Hams. Varieties here include Tom Putt, Fairmaid of Devon and Slack Ma Girdle. It is under these trees that the village holds its annual Twelfth Night wassail. As a part of the revelry, the wassail queen (chosen from year six of the local primary school) pours cider around the apple trees to ensure next year's harvest.

More ancient still is the yew which spreads its venerable branches on crutches over much of the churchyard next door. The tree is thought to be between 1200 and 1400 years old. Be sure to walk around the trunk three

ORCHARDS

The delightfully named Slack Ma Girdle was one of many apple varieties which grew in the orchards which until quite recently lined the Dart Valley. Apple orchards were a common sight all over the South Hams, and it was not until after the second world war that they began to disappear. It is said that ninety percent of South Hams' orchards have been lost since 1945.

Back in the early nineties, the Coast and Countryside Service began a strenuous campaign to conserve the few orchards that remained and to plant new ones. Local campaigners have saved many unique apple varieties localised to a village, or even to one farm. These include the Totnes Apple, Greasy Butcher, Chadders and Ironside (all found near Salcombe), and Browns of Staverton.

Apple Day—Common Ground's inspired invention—is celebrated with gusto each October, and there are community apple pressing days for growers, as well as an advice service, newsletter and stall in the Farmer's Market in Kingsbridge which sells local apples.

For more information contact Orchard Link, P O Box 109, Totnes, Devon TQ9 5XR ☎ 01803 861183.

times backwards to make a wish come true. Another must is to search out the mummified cat over a pint in the dark-beamed Church House Inn, or on returning to the quay, stop for tea and a wedge of home-made cake at the waterside Quayhole Café.

Walk 5: A circular walk & ferry into town from Little Dartmouth

Parking can be tricky in Darmouth, so why not make a leisurely day of it and take an uplifting circular route which follows clifftop meadows on the outward journey and a spectacular stretch of coastal path on the way back. In all the journey is around 3 miles.

The walk starts from the National Trust Car park at Redlap, following the bridleway through Little Dartmouth Farm. This high-sided lane occasionally reveals deep views out to sea through farm gateways. The lane ends at a gate, which leads into a field. Pass through a second gate on to a lane, past the coastguard cottages. The lane drops downhill to Compass Cottage. From here continue downhill to a flight of steps to your right. It is from the bottom of the castle steps that the foot ferry runs into the town centre during the summer months.

Make the most of the refreshment the town has to offer. If you really want to push the boat out, try tapas and cava at Browns Hotel in Victoria

SLOE GIN

Pick the sloes in winter after the first frosts. They should be plump and a dull purplish black. Wash them, then either prick each sloe with a pin several times—or cheat, and put them in the freezer overnight then defrost.

Measure out 12 oz white sugar to each pound of sloes, and put in a wide mouthed jar. Top up with a pint of gin. Put in a cool place, and up-end the jar occasionally to dissolve the sugar. Ready for drinking in about two to three months, but tastes better when kept for a year or more. Sloe gin is a dark carmine colour, and has a rich warming flavour.

Road, or a glass of champagne and olives in the sleek surroundings of Bakers Bar a few doors down. On the other hand, if the weather is fine, a fresh crab sandwich from the Crabshell in Raleigh Street on a bench by the river is hard to beat.

When the town has been thoroughly explored, return by foot ferry to the castle steps. Retrace the route to Compass Cottage and take the lower fork in the track. Follow the coast path through shady woodland onto an open path. This crosses the top of a rock platform—a favoured picnic place—then crosses a small bridge over a deep rock chasm. Before Compass Cove the path veers away from the sea, and climbs steeply up to a high clifftop level from where you look down on to the backs of flying birds.

In Autumn, along this stretch of the walk you may find big juicy sloe berries (see above). The last stretch of the footpath turns inland alongside fields back to the car park.

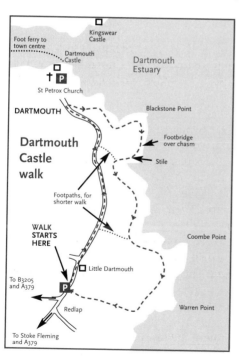

Foot ferry to town centre

Kingswear Castle

Dartmouth Castle

Dartmouth Estuary

St Petrox Church

DARTMOUTH

Blackstone Point

Dartmouth Castle walk

Footbridge over chasm

Stile

Footpaths, for shorter walk

WALK STARTS HERE

Coombe Point

Little Dartmouth

To B3205 and A379

Redlap

Warren Point

To Stoke Fleming and A379

Dittisham

The Lord's my Shepherd,
  I'll not want,
He maketh me down to lie.
In pastures green
He leadeth me
The quiet waters by.

[Written by Rev. Francis Rous,
born in Dittisham c.1600]

Dittisham is built around a promontory three miles upstream from Dartmouth. Houses tumble down the hill to a rocky waterfront, where lines of boats flap around the pier and jetty. The village stands on a bend in the river, close to a stretch of water known as the Dittisham Lake, where at high tide the river is almost a mile across to Galmpton on the far shore. Such a wondrous setting has led to houses being acquired by the very rich, many being used for second homes. Local families have had to retreat to the more affordable margins of the village.

The Domesday survey records the village as Didashim—meaning homestead of Deedas, who was thought to have been a Saxon leader around 660 AD. The Black Death, which was first reported in Devon in 1349, struck Dittisham very hard, and large numbers of victims were buried there—Dittisham has had a burial ground for at least a thousand years, with around 18,000 people believed to be interred around the parish. From the ancient church of St George at Dittisham there are far-reaching views of the river and surrounding countryside, and beside the church are some of the oldest cottages in the village. Dittisham has some fine exam-

ples of traditional local architecture, with stone and cob cottages beneath thatched or local slate rooves. Elderly stone walls hung with gardens of wildflowers, and ancient hedgerows, flank the snaking village lanes.

In spring, Dittisham was once buried beneath blossom which foamed from the many plum and damson orchards. The village even had its own species of plum, thought to have been introduced to the village by visiting German

Dittisham from the river / Dittisham Mill Creek

sailors. Sadly, many of those orchards have been grubbed up, but in late July the few trees which survive still produce fruit, which can be seen for sale in baskets on the occasional doorstep.

Whether crabbing from the jetty, pausing for a drink at the Ferry Boat Inn, or simply waiting for the foot ferry, the quay is a perfect place to idle away the time. The water bubbles with activity. Dittisham has its own yacht club, sailing school and annual regatta, which is held at the end of July or beginning of August. The Ham car park has direct access to the water for launching small craft. At the top of the village is the **Red Lion Inn**. This pub, favoured by the locals, has a good children's room and is very popular for Sunday lunches. The village shop next door is well stocked for everyday needs, and also sells a good selection of local produce. **The Red Lion Inn, The Level, Dittisham ☎ 01803 722235.**

The Ferry Boat Inn, on the river front, is a good stopping place for winter walkers. It has a lovely open fire, spectacular views, and serves large and oozy brie and mushroom baguettes at lunchtime. **The Ferry Boat Inn, Manor Street, Dittisham ☎ 01803 722368.**

Anchorstone Café At the end of WWII the first aid centre on the banks of the Dart at Dittisham was turned into a café, and it has stayed that way ever since. It is now the Anchorstone Café, run by Clare Harvey and family. Serving breakfast, lunch, tea, and, in the season, early evening meals made with fresh local ingredients, the Anchorstone is perfect for families. It has an awning for the outdoor eating area on drizzly days, and outdoor heaters for the chilly ones. Helen serves delicious salads, platters of local cheeses and seafood fresh off the boats. Talking of which, Helen's daughter Jasmine teaches sailing at Dittisham. Ask at the café for details. **Anchorstone Café, Manor Street, Dittisham ☎ 01803 722365.**

The Dittisham and Cornworthy area is laced with craftspeople of one sort or another. Beavering away in their homes and workshops, it is only on occasions that their work becomes visible. An annual craft fair takes place before Christmas, at which the standard of work is exceptionally high. Keep an eye on the noticeboards for such events or exhibitions.

Crux Craft Fair Watch out for the Crux Craft Fair, which takes place around the end of November. It's a rare chance to see the work of a select group of local artists, craftsmen and women in one fell swoop. The atmos

DEVON'S DEEP LANES

The first thing that will strike you about south Devon is the deep and narrow hedged lanes, which twist and turn. Not built for cars, Devon lanes were made by and for packhorses, and by respecting everyone's landholding, they got travellers from A to B in a rather roundabout way.

On narrow 'green lanes' that haven't been widened for cars, you can still see the ridges in the hedgebanks made by generations of wooden pack saddles forcing their way through. With no surfacing, heavy winter rain and fertile soils, these lanes became pools of mud, and had to be regularly scraped back to a harder surface (the mud being dumped on either side), thus creating or deepening the 'Devon banks'. In coastal areas, these deep lanes had their own advantages, and the locals made them deeper still—to hide the packhorses, and people carrying smuggled goods, from the customs men.

The ridge roads—for example the road that runs from the coast near Slapton past East Allington, through Moreleigh, Diptford and on to the south side of Dartmoor—were used for driving sheep up on to moorland grazing for the summer months. Young men would stay with the flocks on the moor for perhaps three or four months before returning to winter in the sheltered valleys of the South Hams.

Typical Devon green lanes

phere is warm and buzzy, and it's a chance to consider Christmas in good time. The range of work on sale is wide: There's Peet Leather's exuberant felt hats, Gilly James's patchwork cushions, and the work of printmakers Susan Deakin, Louise Scammell and Linda Looker. Ironwork by Spencer Field Larcombe and those baskets of desire made by Hilary Burns and Sarah Pank. Guelder rose jelly, hedgelayer's jam and cider apple jelly are just some of Deb Ingram's pretty preserves, each with a hand-designed and coloured label. Mike Ingram's walking sticks—it's impossible to resist touching them—are made from locally coppiced wood.

Set aside at least a couple of hours for your visit, and tarry awhile for (no ordinary) coffee and cake or a main meal at the café. Note: the venue can change. Last year it was Harberton village hall that hummed for the weekend. **Contact Hilary Burns ☎ 01803 553144.**

Bridget McCrum's Garden Dittisham is the home of sculptor Bridget McCrum. For two weekends in May, her riverside garden is open to the public as part of the National Gardens Scheme. The sculptures are an integral part of this garden, which is more to do with uplifting walks and enjoyment of space and form than drifts of flowers.

To Greenway Gardens by foot and ferry

When the National Trust acquired what once was crime novelist Agatha Christie's garden, they set themselves the task of encouraging at least 40 percent of visitors to arrive on foot or by ferry. This journey does just that, combining foot travel with a ferry trip and getting to see both faces of the lower Dart in so doing. From Dartmouth catch David Ridalls' open boat to Dittisham, and the foot ferry will take you across the river to Greenway. Alight at the tiny quay, and make your way uphill to the gardens. The entrance fee is reduced for 'on foot' visitors. The garden is still being revealed and conserved by the Trust, and exploring the paths that zigzag through it is quite an adventure. It dates back to 1547, when Sir Walter Raleigh's step-brother used Armada prisoners to landscape the riverside paths and establish camellia walks. However, the gardens as we see them today were largely established at the turn of the century by the Williams family, who were well-known plant collectors. The garden is filled with rare trees and shrubs from their time there.

March and April is the time to catch the tulip trees and other early spring shrubs in flower. The Hicks—the previous owners of the gardens—are responsible for a rare collection of southern hemisphere plants, including the Chilean Flame trees which burn brightly in June.

The old barn houses a café which serves light lunches, and delicious cakes. Upstairs is a gallery area which hosts the work of local artists. The café is open to all, but if coming by car, a place must be reserved in the car park.

The return journey to Dartmouth on foot covers about four miles. It begins at Greenways' small car park. Follow the Dart Valley Trail's waymarks through the fields to emerge behind Maypool—an imposing Edwardian house, now a youth hostel—then follow the trail up a track which will lead into Long Wood. The moist, warm conditions of the valley make this oak wood drip with polypody, ferns and lichens. Steam trains puff between the woodland and the river's edge. The trail eventually emerges at the top of the road which leads down to the higher ferry which crosses the river back to Dartmouth. Greenway Gardens is open from Wednesday to Saturday, March to October. **Greenway Gardens National Trust ☎ 01803 842382, David Ridalls ☎ 0781 8001108.** For other 'green ways' to Greenway call the National Trust number listed above.

Cornworthy

The village of Cornworthy is almost lost between the hills that surround it. The dark stone buildings give it a rather serious air (stone quarried from Cornworthy was used in the building of Dartmouth Castle). It still has the atmosphere of a working village, and although it recently lost its shop, the pub—the **Hunters Lodge Inn**—is very much alive. Outside the church of St Peter is a splendid old oak tree; inside is the parish book, which allows the visitor a privileged insight into the village. A leaflet has also been produced which details waymarked walks in the parish (available in the Hunters Lodge Inn).

Cornworthy Priory In a field a quarter of a mile to the west of the village stands the remains of the double-entranced gatehouse of Cornworthy Priory. Mounds in the surrounding fields mark where its walls once stood. Dedicated to St Mary, the priory was founded for a small community of Augustinian

A DEVONSHIRE DOZEN

It was the practice in Devon to make cloth in its own peculiar dimensions: 12 yards long and one yard wide—a Devonshire Dozen.

nuns around 1230. Records of the priory are fragmented, but by 1461 it seems the nuns had become a little slack in their religious observations. An admonitory letter from Bishop John Vesey at his Chudleigh palace to the Prioress Avis Dynham implies that life at the Priory must have become far too secular. He instructed them henceforth not to dress in pompous apparel, to sleep in the one dormitory and to eat together, listening to the 'complative lectour', to refrain from meddling in outside husbandry and wandering in the fields and other profane places. They were forbidden to receive sojourners, and were to remove within one month all the servants not necessary for the place.

Fifteen years later, Henry VIII's commissioners arrived to assess the value of the convent's possessions; the dissolution of all the religious houses was complete by 1539. Pinned to the gate beside the ruin is a hand-painted sign directing the visitor to the source of Priory Spring Water.

Carpenter Oak is an architectural service based in East Cornworthy, which specialises in crucked oak barn structures, built in the traditional manner by a team of skilled carpenters. Along the road between Dittisham and Cornworthy, two Carpenter Oak buildings are visible: one is at Lamper Head, on high ground above the river, and another can be seen close by Dittisham Mill Creek (the home of kingfishers). These are very successful examples of 'bungalow eating',

> ### FROM CRADLE TO COFFIN
>
> The most we collect from a hedgerow now is probably a few blackberries in autumn. Years ago, many farm labourers were 'given' a length of hedge to manage and use—hence the hedges were kept in good repair. In laying a hedge you could take out firewood, coppice ash and hazel, cut lengths for tool handles, and let a few mature trees grow for your old age. When cut, they would provide saleable timber, some wood to carve for furniture—for a grandchild's cradle or for your own coffin.

Carpenter Oak building at Dittisham Mill Creek

whereby the oak additions have devoured an unremarkable bungalow bit by bit, transforming it into a building of architectural merit. **Carpenter Oak Ltd, Longlands Workshop, East Cornworthy ☎ 01803 732900.**

Produce, Crafts and Makers

Between East Cornworthy and Dittisham, in the village of Capton, is the workshop of blacksmith **John Churchill**, who produces hand-made architectural and domestic ironmongery. A visit is strongly recommended. His unfussy collection of latches, catches, poles, stays, hooks and handles are a breath of fresh air. John Churchill's commissions have included weather-vanes, gates, staircases and metal stepping-stones. Visit by appointment. **John Churchill, Smith Cottage, Capton ☎ 01803 712535.**

Tideford Organics make fresh soups and sauces cooked from seasonal ingredients and hermetically sealed in chunky glass jars. The soups and sauces change from season to season. These may be sweet potato and sweetcorn chowder, Pommoburro (a delicious buttery tomato and basil sauce), Spinach and dahl soup, Moroccan lamb soup, and there's those Hey Pesto's—the latest one is Porcini. Phone for local stockists, or you can buy direct from Tideford by mail order. **Tideford Organic Foods ☎ 01803 712387. www.tidefordfoods.co.uk.**

Coombe Farm Studios Paul and Tina Riley have run art and craft courses from Coombe since 1982. The converted stone barns assembled round a courtyard provide a wonderful environment for living and working. There is also an exhibition space which shows work by makers, predominantly from the Westcountry. Paul Riley's vibrant and accomplished watercolours are an inspiration to any student. Other courses run here include pottery, papier maché, printmaking, jewellery and indigo dyeing. Friends and family may accompany students on a bed and breakfast basis, and group bookings are welcomed. **Coombe Farm Studios, Dittisham ☎ 01803 722352. Gallery open Mon–Sat 10 am–5 pm.**

Fingals Being a guest at Fingals is a bit like dropping in on a house-party. Meals are lengthy, sociable affairs, in which a restricted choice of dishes ensures absolute freshness. Fingals welcomes casual walkers for a cup of tea or a drink. There is an ease about the place, which is scattered with generous flourishes from the owners Richard and Sheila Johnston, who somehow manage to give the impression that running such a fabulous spread is quite without effort. **Fingals, Old Coombe Manor Farm, Dittisham ☎ 01803 722398.**

Bow Creek

Upriver from Dittisham is Bow Creek, which stretches for a mile until it reaches the village of Tuckenhay. Disused quays and warehouses are left as reminders of past trading from the village—cider was once shipped to London from here, as was stone for road-making. The village manufactured gas, which was used for lighting as early as 1806. It also had two paper mills, one of which (Arthur Millbourn and Co) continued to make finest quality paper until the 1970s.

The Maltsters A glorious situation beside the creek, a great ambience, and good food are three reasons to visit the Maltsters. It also has the plus of being hospitable to both dogs and children, for whom there is a menu (the children, that is) which for once doesn't assume under twelves to have palates of polystyrene. **The Maltsters Arms, Tuckenhay ☎ 01803 732350.**

Sharpham

The Sharpham Estate offers a diverse range of activities to local people and visitors, and may be reached by foot or by bicycle along the cycle path from Totnes via Ashprington or by river from Dartmouth, Dittisham or Totnes.

Sharpham House is built on a plateau above the River Dart, and sheltered by hills and woods behind. The rebuilding of the house as we see it today began in the 1770s and was completed 50 years later. The existing Elizabethan house was incorporated into the new design by Robert Taylor, architect of the Bank of England. Sharpham House was designed in the neo-classical Palladian style, but because the ground around the house sloped so steeply it wasn't possible to have the main entrance opening onto a fashionable

Sharpham Boathouse with Vineyard beyond

grand portico with roof-supporting pillars. Instead Taylor decided to place the portico inside the hallway, creating an octagonal hall with eight supporting pillars. This led to a larger hall and the main staircase which Anne Bancroft describes in her informative and detailed booklet 'Sharpham House: A Short History':

"Taylor's delight was mathematics, and nowhere better can this be seen than in the staircase. Here the long stone slabs forming the steps are let into the wall by only two inches and have no outer support to bring them to the horizontal. The trick was to place them at such an angle that they were supported by the torsion of the curves, like an arch laid on its side, although when it came to the landings—looming outwards with nothing beneath—his genius was surely exceptional."

In 1962 Maurice and Ruth Ash bought the Sharpham estate. Ruth Ash had spent her childhood locally at Dartington Hall, bought by her parents Leonard and Dorothy Elmhirst in 1925. They formed a charitable Trust in 1984 and over the years Sharpham has become a centre for a diversity of projects which seek to balance practical endeavour with spiritual enquiry. When Maurice Ash died in 2003, the house passed to the Sharpham Trust.

The Sharpham Trust runs a number of charitable activities, which include:

The Sharpham Centre for Contemporary Buddhist Enquiry, offering courses, lectures and public events. These are publicised through their programme, on the website or locally on posters in the town. **Sharpham Centre for Contemporary Buddhist Enquiry ☎ 01803 732542, email centre@sharpham-trust.org.**

The Barn, a working rural retreat centre, provides the opportunity to retreat, meditate, take part in cooperative living, and work in Sharpham's productive organic garden. **Barn Rural Retreat ☎ 01803 732661 barn@sharphamcollege.org.**

Sharpham Outdoors offers environmentally themed activities and projects to children, young people and adults. Look out for the community willow bed open days; monthly Wildlife Watch group meetings for children aged 8–14 years; workshops on environmental art and family bush-craft

CHARCOAL MAKING

Gather a few pencil size willow sticks into a bunch. Wrap them in foil. Seal tightly. Place in the hot embers of a fire for 10–15 minutes. Cool and unwrap. Perfect charcoal for drawing.

days which may involve the building of shelters, foraging for food, making fires and cooking on them. Sharpham Outdoors is led by the Trust's Education Ranger, Catherine White, who also works with local schools, community organisations and carers. For details contact **Sharpham Outdoors ☎ 01803 732799, email ranger@sharpham-trust.org.** Public events are listed in the AONB Service's Coast and Countryside events programme and on the Sharpham Trust website at **www.sharpham-trust.org.**

The Sharpham Partnership, a tenant of the Trust, produces a range of artisan wines and cheeses with an excellent reputation (see next page).

The two other farms on the estate are also of interest: Upper Sharpham Barton Bio-dynamic Farm, which runs a regular family camp during August; and the Robert Owen Community Farm at Lower Sharpham Barton (see box below).

ROBERT OWEN COMMUNITY FARM

Around a mile and a half out of Totnes along the cycle track to Ashprington, where the river has broken its banks into marshland, watch out for a stone gate with an old farm track leading up the hill. Around 200m up the track is Lower Sharpham Barton Farm, part of the Sharpham Trust which is farmed by the Robert Owen Foundation. All the day-to-day tasks on this organic farm are undertaken by small groups of adults with special needs under the supervision of members of staff. Sheep, cattle pigs and poultry are all farmed at Lower Sharpham Barton, and on Friday afternoons between 2.00 and 4.30 the farm-yard is open to the public to sell its produce. Organic beef, lamb and pork are on sale most weeks, as well as free range eggs and green top milk (luxuriantly creamy and with that old fashioned 'top of the milk' still intact.)

If making your way by road from Totnes, turn left at the crossroads before Ashprington, after 50m turn right, continue down the hill over the speedbumps and turn left into the farmyard.

Lower Sharpham Barton Farm ☎ 01803 732502.

Catherine White, Education Ranger, Sharpham Outdoors

Cheese and Wine

It was Maurice Ash who first decided to grow grape vines on the south-facing slopes beside the River Dart and to produce cheeses from the doe-eyed Jersey cows that graze the fields at Sharpham. The sheltered position and tidal waters of the river create a mild microclimate, and this together with the red shillet soils and skilful choice of grape varieties has yielded some outstanding wines. Grapes grown include Madelaine Angevine, Kernling Phoenix Dornfelder and Pinot Noir. Both new world and traditional techniques are used in the winery. Dart Valley Reserve 2003 is a very popular off-dry white wine made from a blend of different grape varieties. The flavour is described as supple and delicate with fruity aromas. The Sharpham Red 2003 is described as the colour of garnet with flavours 'intense and lingering' and tastes of raspberry damson and ripe berry fruit. Cheeses from the dairy are produced by traditional methods entirely by hand. Sharpham, a Coloummier-type cheese, has been made to the dairy's own recipe since 1980. The only additions to the fresh Jersey milk are starter cultures, vegetable rennet and salt. Then there is the Rustic, a semi-hard cheese with a rich creamy texture, and the fresh curd cheese Santa Lucia, which is only on sale at the Sharpham shop during the summer.

Guided and self-guided tours are available around the vineyards, and it its possible to view the different stages of cheesemaking through strate-gically placed viewing windows. **Information on tours and shop ☎ 01803 732203.**

The Café

After cycling from Totnes, rowing from Dartmouth or simply ambling down from the car park, there is sustenance at hand—between May and September, that is. The café at Sharpham may look a little unsophisti-cated, but the food that Rosie Weston manages to produce from her trailer is very very good. She uses the cheese from the dairy, and vegeta-bles and salad from the walled garden up the hill. Rosie maintains it is the short distance that the food travels that makes it tastes so delicious, but I suspect it has something to do with her culinary know-how. This is al fresco eating, and on a small scale. There are ten tables on the deck, and possibly a marquee. If it's busy, be prepared for a wait, for everything is cooked to order. A plate of Sharpham cheese with spelt bread and a glass of Dart Valley Reserve, overlooking the river—it can't be bad. **The Café ☎ 07790 474319.**

Totnes

The river remains navigable up to the weir at Totnes. The first road bridge across the Dart links Totnes to Bridgetown, on the east side of the water.

A brief history

At a time when Vikings were paddling their way up every waterway in Devon, seizing who or whatever were in their way, Edward, elder son of Alfred the Great, was scouring the South Hams for sites to build his planned series of fortified towns as a defence against the ravages of the Danes. It was beside a fordable stretch of the River Dart near the main highway to Plymouth that Edward came across a steeply rising promontory. This he judged to be an ideal situation for one such town; plentiful fishing, fertile soil and and a fine lookout point at the top of the hill. Edward lost no time in calling in the King's men to build the walled town upon the hill which was named Totnes [*Tot* = lookout, and *ness* or *naise* = nose]. This was the early 900s. It is still possible to make out the original Saxon boat-shaped town of Totnes from the air, with tenements bordering the main street, and behind them long narrow garden strips (burghage plots) which stretched all the way to the town walls.

It was two hundred years later that Totnes Castle was built by Judhael—a Breton who had been given the town as a gift from William the Conqueror. He built the castle with forced labour, in so doing flattening the original settlement which had clustered upon the volcanic tip of the hill. Gradually, as the threat of invasion subsided, people risked building their homes closer and closer to the River Dart, which was the centre for

trading cloth, leather and slate. It was cloth that became a major part of the town's economy; in 1253 'Totnes russet' had been chosen for the King's bed. The industry employed a large percentage of the Totnes workforce—family names associated with the cloth trade, such as Fuller, Tucker and Dyer, are still common locally. Cloth production went through many stages: by the time the cloth reached the

High Street, Totnes

public space where it was stretched on tenter hooks, it had passed through the homes of both spinners and weavers as well as the waterside tucking mills. The speed at which the plague coursed through Totnes, wiping out two-thirds of the town, was thought to be to do with the many hands the cloth passed through during its manufacture.

By the 1500s, the Totnes merchants' overseas trade was flourishing. The second richest town in Devon, Totnes was also benefitting from trading in tin from Dartmoor. This rise in fortunes brought substantial development to the town. A rash of new buildings sprang up, and existing houses were fundamentally revamped to keep abreast of fashion. By the end of the century there were as many as fifty new fashioned gable houses with timber-framed oriel windows. The peak of Totnes's fortunes was reached in the early 1600s, after which came a steady decline. By the 1700s the movers and shakers had moved on to more happening places, leaving behind them a staid population remarkable only for its community of clockmakers. It had become little more than a rural market town, a pleasant place to live, particularly for large families with small estates—for produce was both abundant and cheap. Building had more or less ceased with this decline in fortunes and it is thanks to the fact that Totnes was never again so economically buoyant that contemporary Totnes is falling over itself in superb examples of 16th and 17th century architecture with all its attendant plasterwork, courtyards and decorative slate tiles. In fact, the town boasts the highest incidence of listed buildings per head of population in Britain.

Tudor houses of note in the town can be found at 52 & 54 High Street, 20 High Street, and 70 Fore Street (The Museum). Good examples of plasterwork are seen at 16 High Street (Nicholas Ball's

Details of houses in Totnes town centre / Atherton Passage

house), 64 Fore Street, and the Council
Chamber in the Guildhall.

Lesser notables of Totnes include
Edward Lye, compiler of the first Anglo-
Saxon dictionary; and Benjamin Kennicot,
compiler of the 'Hebrew Old Testament
with various readings'.

Alternative Totnes—the Seeds

It was in the early 1800s when the first recorded attempt to put Totnes on
the map as a centre for alternative health was made. A nameless entrepreneur made an attempt to market the medicinal waters from the Leech
Wells. These waters, it was claimed, cured plague as well as curing skin
disorders. Perhaps this was just an idea ahead of its time, for Totnes failed
in its attempt to become a spa town and settled back into rural quiescence.

Entertainment

Diversions in the town took on various forms at different times. Bulls
were baited on The Plains before and after church, and bowls were rolled
on St Peter's Quay. Theatricals were played in assorted venues, including
the theatre above No. 28 High Street. Just opposite, there was a cockpit.

The Totnes Races galloped on to the scene just
before 1800, with large crowds gathering on the
marshes to see the horses charge across the river
and up into the farthest reaches of Bridgetown.

The coming of Dorothy and Leonard Elmhirst to
Dartington in 1925 had a profound effect upon the
locality. Leonard's ideal of creating a self-sufficient
rural community, together with Dorothy's commit-
ment to the arts, brought an injection of new energy
to the area. Pioneers in all these fields visited or
worked in Dartington. Followers settled in neighbouring villages as well as in Totnes, in order to
participate in what were undeniably exciting times.
Before long, Totnes emerged as a thriving centre for
alternative living. This has its advantages, for
concentrated into the Totnes area is an extraordinary
number of activities, businesses & events servicing
the needs of alternative culture.

The Clock Tower from the High Street

Totnes

Art and Crafts

Totnes has a wealth of craftspeople living and working around the area: it would need a whole book to cover the subject properly. Some need seeking out, and others have outlets in local shops. A list of members of **The Devon Guild of Craftsmen** is available through their website which links to images of the individual artists' work. **www.devonguild-ofcraftsmen.co.uk**

Totnes Open Studios

Discover the back doubles of Totnes in search of art. For a week in late spring, the artists' community of the town throw open the doors of their homes and studios to the public. It's a chance to meet the artists and craftspeople in their places of work—which can be anything from a lean-to kitchen to a purpose-built studio. This informal way of showing work is becoming increasingly popular in the South Hams. Similar events take place in Harbertonford and Blackawton. Details of Totnes Open Houses available from **Totnes Tourist Information Centre, The Town Mill ☎ 01803 863168.**

The craftspeople featured below reflect the huge and changing range of arts and crafts represented in the town. They are all in easy walking distance of each other.

Prismatic This craft co-operative sells high-quality work by Devon's craftsmen and women. Sumptuous devoré scarves and clothes by Caroline Hall, and understated jewellery by Jamie Ingliss, are just some of the works on sale in this tiny showroom. **Prismatic, 51 Fore Street.** Open Mon–Sat 10 am–5 pm.

Fifth Element Trevor Forrester's contemporary jewellery can be seen here. If you want a very special ring, Trevor specialises in individually cast wedding and engagement rings, as well as delicate silver tiaras. **Fifth Element, 3 Civic Hall Shops, Market Square ☎ 01803 840740.** Tuesday–Thursday 10–5 Friday & Saturday 9–5.

Shoes

Conker Shoes Conkers wide-toed colourful footwear has become almost a trademark for Totnes. Founded in 1977 by Andy Langford, Conker Shoes now produces over 100 pairs of handmade shoes a week, with a choice of cleated crepe tyre or wedge soles. And when well loved shoes wear out they can be rebuilt for around half the cost of a new pair. Alongside the classically simple leather bags and belts is a selection of unusual women's clothes: the gorgeously detailed Paris-made Solola tops and shirts, the cool Natural Wave German linen, sporty and practical Line 7 from New Zealand, and deliciously soft knitwear by Nazarmi Chiatti. **Conker Shoe Co, 28 High Street ☎ 01803 862490. info@conkershoes.com**

Green Shoes As I write, the makers of handmade women's shoes, Green Shoes, are planning to move from their retail premises in the High Street to a larger workshop in Buckfastleigh, where they will continue their trade over the internet. Around since the early eighties, the no-nonsense, blunt-toed, flat-heeled styles are designed for supreme comfort. It will still be possible to visit the workshop to see and feel the different styles of this enduring footwear for yourself. **www.greenshoes.co.uk**

Paper

Paperworks Sometimes humorous, and occasionally sumptuous, it's the fabulous papery displays in the window at

Totnes

Paperworks which stop people in their tracks. The shop itself is a source of the gorgeous hand-made papers from India, Nepal, Thailand, Japan, and even Wookey Hole. There are also writing instruments, paper flowers, rubber stamps, paper crafts and hand-made albums. **Paperworks, 63 High Street ☎ 01803 867009.**

Miscellaneous

Gazebo "Anyone who tells you money can't buy you happiness just doesn't know where to shop"— advice dispensed from one of the many diverting cards on sale in Gazebo. And it is hard not to feel cheered in this store in the Narrows, amongst a proliferation of the flowery, the feathery, the twinkly, the spotty, the sparkly and the pink. With so much to see, I sought guidance from Helen in between serving

customers. First I was shown an intriguing plastic knicker-hanger trimmed with roses, then the sparkly loo seats, the hula girl trays, colourful Mexican oilcloth, magical fairy tale snowstorms. and a wind-up Jesus. Then came the photographic wall paper: lurid 1960s landscape photographs entitled 'highland falls', 'lakeside mountains' and 'palm-fronded lagoon'. Your chosen scene will be reproduced to fit the exact dimensions of the wall of your choice. Immensely popular—and as seen in the Big Brother bedroom.

The brash and the kitsch is tempered by a demure collection of Cath Kidston crockery, linen and accessories. Then there's the baby stuff. If you haven't a baby to buy for, you'll need to invent one: Tiny tiger shoes in the softest of leather, sky blue bibs printed with billowing clouds. Baby-gros covered in red rose prints or candied paisleys, and for the boys, a camouflage romper suit.

Lastly, Helen's favourite—the magic candle. A pink plastic flower bud which when lit, shoots up a spectacular flame about nine inches high. The flower then opens to reveal seven smaller candles burning, accompanied by the tune

of 'Happy Birthday'. And all for £3.50. **Gazebo, 74 High Street ☎ 01803 863679.**

Textiles

Sally Carr has swept away any reminder of the dry stuffy pastel cardie wool shops of yesteryear. Instead, there are gorgeous yarns, and a rail of irresistible hand-made jackets, jumpers and cardigans. Everything for the adventurous and luxurious knitter. There's also a knitting-up service for those half-knitted jumpers tucked away in a drawer. **Sally Carr Designs, 31 High Street ☎ 01803 863060.**

Greenfibres It's the aroma of natural fibres that hit you from the reams of organic hemp, cotton, linen, and untreated silk on the shelves of Greenfibres' shop near the top of The Narrows. The eco goods and garments sold here have been produced in ways that do not harm the environment or exploit the people who manufacture them, so there's every good reason to buy. Their mail order catalogue is exceedingly seductive for those who delight in the soft, pure and natural. How could babies wear anything other than the softest cotton underwear, completely untreated and

Gazebo in The Narrows

Totnes

undyed? And the Alpaca socks are utterly indulgent. As for the duvets—organic cotton covered and filled with cashmere—heaven! **Greenfibres, 99 High Street ☎ 01803 868001 www.greenfibres.com.**

Stone Fabrics and Sewing Surgery Jane Starey got fed up with trekking up to London every time she needed fabrics. Her daughters badgered her into doing something about it, and she opened her fabric shop and surgery in 1997. Specialising in natural silk and linens, high-tech fabrics including fleece, designer cashmeres and wools, Stone Fabrics has a fabulous selection to choose from. Period buttons are a speciality, with an unusual range that is expanding all the time. Jane also runs regular sewing surgeries for lapsed dressmakers and beginners. Classes are small. Jane also offers a dressmaking service. **Stone Fabrics and Sewing Surgery, 97 High Street ☎ 01803 868608.**

Clothes
Combining designer with art deco, Totnes locals display an eclectic style of dressing—fearless colour combinations, or catholic mixes of ancient and

modern. A sartorial stroll up the High Street includes:
Fusion Kangaroo Poo fleeces and Plain Lazy tees for the urban surfer, plus pointy hemmed velvet skirts for the tasteful hippie. **Fusion, 73 Fore Street ☎ 01803 864204.**
Diva offers a calm space in which to try Noa Noa, Naughty, Diesel, Nicole Farhi, Jackpot or French Connection Lines thoughtfully grouped in blocks of colour. Help is on hand to put it all together. **Diva, 55a High Street ☎ 01803 866528.**
The Foredeck has two shops in Totnes: one young and surfy, one grown up smart casual with lots of bare wood and indigo. Sailing(ish) gear with attitude as well as quality and some striking jewellery. **The Foredeck, 3 High Street ☎ 01803 847848, 37 High Street ☎ 01803 847890.**

Fab Just around the bend in The Narrows is Fab for Women. To the front of the shop are the rails crammed with unusual women's clothes—dominated by labels from the Netherlands—and at the back are the accessories: frivolous shoes, serious boots, cuddly socks, lacy

underwear and wild handbags. A tonic if you're feeling jaded by the lacklustre sameness of the high street chains. And very real prices. Fab for Men is further down the hill, and at Fab for Beauty in Fore Street they give beauty treatments upstairs. **Fab for Women, 68 High Street ☎ 01803 867656, Fab for Men, 58 High Street ☎ 01803 863311 Fab Beauty, 24 Fore Street ☎ 01803 863265.**

Revival Crammed with sequins, feathers and lace, Revival sells period clothes from the Victorian era to the seventies. They have a good selection of menswear. Costume jewellery, shoes and handbags are snapped up by the young, to cries of 'I had some just like that' from their mums or grannies. **Revival, 64 High Street ☎ 01803 866734.**

Fab for Men in the High Street

Totnes

Salago

Indian clothes, leather goods and cosy slippers are sold on the ground floor of this long-established shop. Upstairs is a thoughtful selection of toys made from wood and wool, not plastic and microchips. There's also a good selection of playing cards and enduring games, for those rare rainy days. **Salago, 51 Old Butterwalk, High Street ☎ 01803 865721.**

Books

The Totnes Bookshop
If you're stuck for what to read, consult the helpful 'staff choice' shelf, where a selection of fiction and non-fiction books are accompanied by personal reviews written by staff. Part of the Dartington Hall Trust, the Totnes Bookshop operates as completely independent booksellers, holding an astonishingly wide range of around 12,000 books. Plenty to choose from, and lots of space within which to do it. In the lower area between the children's books and local guides is an engaging collection of classical, early and world music CDs. Particular care has been taken over their range of children's books and there is a special comfy and safe area for the younger ones. Watch out for the regular and immensely popular book signing evenings— convivial get-togethers where prominent authors discuss their work and sign copies of their latest book. **The Totnes Bookshop, 42 High Street ☎ 01803 863273 www.dartingtonhall.org.uk**

If you've a nose for a second-hand book, Totnes has a good selection. They fill the extensive shelves of **Pedlar's Pack** on The Plains— particularly good for natural history, local interest and gardening. Halfway up the hill is **The Bookshop**, for general interest out-of-print books. Opposite the Civic Square is **Harlequin**, with second-hand and some carefully chosen remaindered books. Finally, at the top of town, is the enduring **Collards** in Castle Street. **Pedlar's Pack Books, 4 The Plains ☎ 01803 866423. The Bookshop, 72 Fore Street ☎ 01803 864088.**

Harlequin, 41 High Street ☎ 01803 866406. B. Collard Secondhand Books, 4 Castle Street ☎ 01548 550246.

Arcturus Books and Crystals For a selection of alternative and complementary health titles, Arcturus Bookshop cuts the mustard. Subjects range from astrology, wicca and eastern religions through bodywork and personal growth. There's also an absorbing noticeboard crammed with the stuff that really only Totnes can offer. Coffee-table reading includes periodicals such as *Kindred Spirit*, *Permaculture* and *Pagan Dream, Shamanism Channelled* and *Earth Mysteries*. **Arcturus, 47 Fore Street ☎ 01803 864363.**

Body and Soul

The Float Centre Upstairs above Arcturus Bookshop is the calming Float Centre. A treatment here can, it is claimed, increase learning potential, improve sports performance, and alleviate aches and pains. 100 lbs of epsom salts is dissolved into 10 gallons of water warmed to body temperature, and the body is entirely supported by water. **The Float Centre, 47 Fore Street ☎ 01803 864363.**

Totnes Bookshop in the High Street

Totnes

In the same building is the **Arcturus Clinic**, where practitioners offer consultations in herbal medicine, shiatsu, psychotherapy, acupressure and homeopathy. **Arcturus Clinic, 47 Fore Street** ☎ 01803 868282.

Drop-in Yoga. Gretchen Faust Kaplan arrived from India via New York, and transformed a rather dark space at the Forge in Collins Road into a warm and light yoga studio. She even moved the front door for good feng shui. For the devoted (and very fit), Gretchen runs regular early morning ashtanga yoga sessions. For the less committed (or available) try one of Gretchen's drop-in yoga sessions. **The Forge, Collins Road** ☎ 01803 867440.

Roma Great haircuts downstairs, deliriously relaxing facials, massages etc upstairs. Roma stocks Clarins, the organic Aveda range of products, and they sell make-up too. **Roma Hairdressing, 44 Fore Street** ☎ 01803 865724.

Natural Health Centre Established back in 1978, the Totnes Natural Health Centre was the first of its kind in the UK. A wealth of different therapists and practitioners work from the centre. Some give treatments for donation; private sessions may be arranged. For relaxing treatments try aromatherapy, reiki, shiatsu or reflexology. **Natural Health Centre, Waterside, The Plains** ☎ 01803 864587.

Food Shops
Ticklemore Cheese Shop This small dairy has an excellent range of local cheeses as well as other British and European ones. Try the Beenleigh Blue, or Sharpham Brie. For the sweet-toothed, there is **Rocombe Dairy** ice cream in many of its delicious flavours. Ticklemore Cheese is a deservedly prize-winning business, supplying some of the best hotels, pubs and restaurants in the locality. **Ticklemore Cheese Shop, 1 Ticklemore Street** ☎ 01803 865926.

Annie's Fruit and Veg Opposite Ticklemore Cheese is Annie's Fruit and Veg. This popular greengrocer sells extremely fresh vegetables and local eggs. The service is fast and helpful, and there's usually some local gossip to be picked up in the queue and sometimes a bunch of cheering anemones grown in Stokeinteignhead. **Annie's Fruit and Veg, Unit 4, Totnes Shopping Centre** ☎ 01803 867265.

Riverford goes to town

Riverford Goes to Town There's always a pot of home-made soup simmering at RGtT at lunchtime, and it's ready to take away with bread baked on the farm that morning. There are also hot pies, pasties, scotch eggs and in summer, lots of fresh salads to try. Riverford Farm Foods bring their scrupulously resourced fresh vegetables, meat, cheeses, preserves, wines, oils and olives to the high street. Much is local, a lot organic, and this is indicated by a helpful blue /green labelling system. Watch out for the South Devon Chilli farm sauces and pickles, and Tyrells colourful root vegetable chips. Bread comes in

Totnes

wheels as well as loaves, and the cheese straws are, by all accounts, addictive. **Riverford Goes to Town, 39 High Street, ☎ 01803 863959 www.-riverfordfarmshop.co.uk**

Sacks Wholefoods Totnes wouldn't be Totnes without Sacks, with its familiar wholefoodie smell and unchanging layout. The mainstay of many a Totnesian, it holds a wide-ranging stock of anything the macrobiotic, vegan or vegetarian might require. Makes a change from Safeways. Prices are good, as is the produce. There is a small (but good) range of organic vegetables, as well as a compelling noticeboard. **Sacks Wholefoods, 80 High Street ☎ 01803 863263.**

Greenlife The ultimate green supermarket. Greenlife's functional interior offers a bewildering choice of wholefoods and natural products. Nine flavours of locally made Dragonfly tofu burgers are next to 19 types of rice cakes. From dried Japanese sea vegetables and Ayurvedic teas which balance your chakras, to a discerning organic wine selection and organic white chocolate ice cream. **Greenlife, 11 Fore Street ☎ 01803 868265.**

Skysprouts In 1986 when the only sprouts we ate were Brussels, personnel at American air bases were snapping up Skysprouts' cartons of live sprouted seeds. Today, they offer a choice of twelve including alfalfa, radish, broccoli and lentil. All organically grown in energised water, they add a protein-packed crunch to salads and sandwiches. Look in Greenlife or Sacks for their sunflower salad, the green shoots set to burst through the lid on to the plate. **Skysprouts ☎ 01364 72404. Products available in Greenlife.**

A.W. Luscombe, Butcher A long-established family business, where meat is unceremoniously hauled down from its hook and cut from the carcass. Luscombes have skilled and helpful butchers who will prepare cuts for you. Suppliers to the best local restaurants, the quality of this meat is exceptional. Be warned: if you ask for a joint for four, you might get rather more than you'd bargained for, as delicate portions aren't the stuff of Luscombes. Game can be ordered. **A.W. Luscombe, 48 Fore Street ☎ 01803 862119.**

Totnes Health Shop Seeds Bakery at Totnes Health Shop sells the most

delicious wholemeal and sunflower loaves of bread. Fresh filled rolls and pies, moist cakes and slices fill their window—it's an ideal place to pick up a picnic. The green bean slice—a surprising combination of red beans pasta and cabbage—should be tried. **Totnes Health Shop, 35 High Street ☎ 01803 862526.**

Effings If you're an olive lover, wait until there's a good long queue to allow maximum tasting time for a wonderful range of olives. This small delicatessen offers an extravagance of continental charcuterie, cheeses and antipasti—perfect to accompany Tom Jaine's glorious bread which is available on occasions. The enthusiastic and knowledgeable team at Effings are happy to advise any wavering or overwhelmed customers. The style of food served in the tiny restaurant is described as fairly eclectic,

Willow Vegetarian Restaurant in The Narrows

Totnes

with an emphasis on southern Europe. I will add that the lunches are supremely good and it is advisable to book. **Effings, 50 Fore Street ☎ 01803 863435.**

Food For Thought Pick up a picnic at Food for Thought. Situated by the old marsh gates on the plains, Food for Thought stocks inventively filled pasties, olive bread, walnut bread, and a great range of tray bakes, all of which (and more) combined to win them a BBC Good Food award. A short walk away is Vire Island, perfect for idle picnicking whilst watching the comings and goings on the river. **Food For Thought, 10 the Plains ☎ 01803 862071.**

Totnes Wine Company This small, privately owned store specialises in small wine estates from the old and the new world's leading regions. Many of the wines on offer can't be found elsewhere in the UK. Plenty of informed advice is always on offer, but if you haven't time to linger a good bet are the house selections, consistent and high quality Claret, White Burgundy and Rioja. **Totnes Wine Company, High Street ☎ 01803 866357. www.totneswine.co.uk** Totnes Market

Totnes draws discerning shoppers, so it follows that the quality of goods on sale at Totnes market is high. In particular, watch out for David Jonas, a fishmonger from East Ogwell selling wet fish fresh from Brixham that morning from his van. He has an excellent selection of local fish— gurnard, john dory, Brixham plaice, ling, whiting, and dabs—at very fair prices. He also has oysters and mussels when in season, and live crabs or—if you're feeling lazy or squeamish—ready prepared ones. In fact he'll prepare any fish for you in the way you want, in seconds. There's always a queue, and the van leaves by twelve o'clock sharp.

Olives can be expensive in delicatessens, and rather dull in supermarkets. The solution: buy from **The Olive Branch**. Sue Prowse made it her business to sell olives and other Mediterranean foods four years ago. She imports Greek, Moroccan and Spanish olives and marinades them at home. A favourite of her Totnes customers are the big fat whole gordal olives. Sue has also sourced some exceptional olive oils— one from a Tuscan mountain village. It comes in two varieties:

the fruity and pungent Intenso made when the olives are still young and green, and the sweeter, more softer Delicato made when the olives are fully ripe and black. Perfect for taking as a gift to a dinner party in place of the bottle of wine. There is so much more to browse on the stall, I recommend see for yourselves or look up the website. **www.-olivebranchdirect.co.uk**

The next stall along sells plants, but no ordinary ones. Lesley Thomas has been coming here for 16 years and is hot wired into the needs of South Hams gardeners. Her most popular shrub is the Muehlenbekia, a modest climber from New Zealand with dark turning stems and tiny leaves. She also specialises in ferns, hellebores, cottage garden perennials and sixteen different varieties of foxglove.

Further into the market square is the **Common Loaf Bakery**, which sells speciality wheat-free breads, including spelt flour—Mediterranean with sun-dried tomato and parmesan, and olive and mixed pepper. Sourdough recipes are also popular, particularly the sunflower and linseed loaf and the 100% rye. And for the sweet tooth, there's fruit bread, spiced fruit buns

Totnes

and blueberry muffins.

Beyond the bread are a cluster of stalls, regular and otherwise, selling colourful clothes, old velvet, recycled furniture, toys, old lace, eastern odds and ends, and jewellery.

Eating Out
Fat Lemons

When I visited Fat Lemons—past the bicycle rickshaw, and through the yellow gates—a powerful wind and diagonal rain had flattened the daffodils on the tables in the little courtyard, and the Mediterranean illusion was hard to maintain. Until, that is, I stepped inside the café where sunny colours, vases of fresh tulips and roses on red gingham, and the smell of aromatic tea and fresh lemons, combined to transport me far deeper south.

A place for the discerning tea drinker, I

counted 77 varieties listed, with intriguing names such as Russian Caravan, China Snail Pekoe and white tea. And if you are indecisive, there is always refreshing home-made lemonade. A good place for unusual breakfasts—organic beans on spelt bread, and mushrooms with tofu. The lunchtime specials are around the seven quid mark—on my visit it was vegetable tagine, and cheesy leek, mushroom, and potato bake. Particular effort is made to accommodate special dietary needs. In Totnes, I am told, there is a growing community of raw food eaters, and others who exclude members of the nightshade family (tomatoes, peppers potatoes) from their diet. With notice, Fat Lemons will come up with something inventive and delicious for, it seems, just about anyone.
**Fat Lemons Café,
1 Ticklemore Court,
Ticklemore Street
☎ 01803 866888.**

Willow Wholefood Vegetarian Restaurant is run by a group of committed pure foodies. Their menu has an excellent selection of imaginative salads all year round. In the back room there's a thoughtful

children's corner, and a rack of ecologically sound mags. Outside in the leafy courtyard there's alfresco dining. Special Willow nights with themed food and music are held regularly. **Willow Wholefood Vegetarian Restaurant, 87 High Street ☎ 01803 862605.**

Rumour Wine Bar A classic wine bar formula, with occasional live music and faithful local support. Besides the *à la carte* menu there are generous bar snacks and wonderful home-made pizzas (with loads of runny toppings) which can be taken out. **Rumour Wine Bar, 30 High Street ☎ 01803 864682.**

The Waterside Bistro and Café
Matt and Delphine Buzzo use the best of local fish, organic meat and vegetables. All the food is freshly prepared, and much made to order. The terrace adjoining the bistro is safely fenced, making it perfect for those with small children. An evening meal in the bistro is a treat. Great care is taken in the cooking, creating considered combinations of taste and texture. It's a peaceful place to eat with intelligent, unobtrusive service. The bright white café with scrubbed wood tables serves, amongst

Fat Lemons Café in Ticklemore Street

Totnes

other things, generous and thoughtful salads, a reassuring fish pie and home-made soup. Pastries, scones and a particularly dark and moist chocolate cake are prepared by the morning pastry chef, and special hot dishes are chalked on the board daily. Both the Bistro and café are non-smoking with disabled access, and both occupy super waterside sites overlooking the river and Vire Island. **Waterside Bistro and Café** ☎ 01803 864069.

Greys Dining Room Immerse yourself in afternoon tea at Greys, with its profusion of painted china and traditional metal teacake warmers. Home-made cakes, a selection of teas and fresh scones all come served in reassuringly cosseted surroundings. **Greys Dining Rooms, 96 High Street** ☎ 01803 866869.

The Barrel House With its dark continental atmosphere, this is the place to catch up on gossip, 'hang out', and meet friends for power breakfasts. At night, convivial diners can be seen from the street. Watch out for the occasional evening showings of local film makers' work—complete with popcorn. **The Barrel House, 59a High Street** ☎ 01803 863000.

The Community Café Eating with toddlers can be tricky, and some cafés don't make it any easier. The Community Café takes it all in its stride, serving homely food at good prices. Housed in what was the old grammar school, it forms part of a busy community centre running dozens of courses and activities. **The Community Café, The Mansion, Fore Street** ☎ 01803 862566.

Places To Visit
Totnes Museum This small museum is housed in a splendid Elizabethan building. Outside is the Tudor herb garden, authentically planted. Beside it there's an amazingly well-stocked community archive and local studies library. The small scale of the museum is perfect for children, who will enjoy the 'nursery', filled with Victorian toys and games. **Totnes Museum, 70 Fore Street** ☎ 01803 863821.

The Guildhall Still used by the Totnes Town Council, the panelled hall with wooden 'throne' seats has seen the inauguration of an awful lot of mayors since 1359. Children will thrill to see the old town cells, peep at the old mayoral robes or hear the tale of the ghost on the stairway. **The Guildhall, Ramparts Walk** ☎ 01803 862147.

WINTER TREATS

The high streets are quiet in January—for many it's time to shut up shop and take a holiday or get the decorators in. Others make it their business to draw in the locals. So watch out for lunch-time deals in restaurants which normally lie outside your budget. Wills in Totnes were offering a mouth-watering three courses at lunch-time, two for the price of one at £19.00, and Restaurant 42 in Salcombe do two meals for £42. Also spas and beauty treatments can be eager for custom at this time of year. It's worth a phone call to check what's on offer, or look in the local paper.

NICOLA'S PICNIC

Nicola Kennedy of Dartington suggests grabbing a sumptuous Friday picnic in Totnes before hitting the beach . . .

You will need to do a little pre-trip preparation along the lines of a cool bag, butter, plates or napkins, cups, knives, and a large thermos of whatever reviving brew takes your fancy. However, the main idea of this picnic is that you just buy your ingredients and head straight for the beach, minimising fuss and maximising pleasure.

This picnic is best assembled on a Friday, because of the market. First make for the fish van and buy prawns. These are iced, and if you put them straight into a cool box will keep well even on a hot beach day. If you are lucky you may also find some smoked roe.

Across the aisle from the fish van, you will find the olive ladies, who will oblige whether your taste runs to the musty, herb-encrusted bitterness of dark black olives, or the lighter fresher taste of green olives marinaded with lemon zest and coriander. You may also want to try some pots of hummus, feta and grilled Mediterranean vegetables.

Further down the aisle is the bread stall. Buy a small or large campagne loaf, depending on the size and appetite of your party, to eat with your prawns. Turn around and head two shops down the hill to 'Riverford Goes to Town', and buy some chocolate brownies. You will be thankful for their sticky sweetness teamed with hot tea when you are shivering on the beach having braved the briny. Placate the children and indulge yourself with a bag of Burt's crisps, and if this is an autumn or spring picnic, grab whatever looks good from their selection of English apples. You may also find some other treats to entice you, such as

smoked guinea fowl breasts, or that clotted cream of cheeses, Sharpham's Elmhirst.

Walk back up the hill to the Happy Apple supermarket and (if it's summer) buy their absolutely ripe-for-eating melons, peaches or nectarines. Look in the chill cabinet and select drinks of organic juices, beer, cider or wine. A robust rosé will certainly help if you are in the mood for a beach-time siesta.

After all that, it's off up the Kingsbridge Hill and simply decide whether you fancy to picnic on the sand and surf of Bantham, or at any of the smaller coves between Gara Rock and Start Point.

Picnicking beside the River Dart

Trips from Totnes

Here are two outings from Totnes. The first takes a trip down Longmarsh beside the river. The second follows the riverside walk and cycle path to Dartington, which links to the Cider Press Craft Centre.

1. A Short Stroll to Longmarsh

For a riverside stroll which is also bike-able, buggyable and wheelchair-friendly, try Longmarsh. Cross Charles Fowler's bridge into Bridgetown (that's what they call the settlement over the water) and take the first road on the right. First right again and you will be heading along Steamer Quay, beside the Dart. Little ones always enjoy spending ages on the wooden play galleon beside the Riverside
Café—but don't let them linger too long; follow the road to the car park, then the path between the river and new marine-inspired industrial units, until you reach the Rowing Club. On early mornings or winter Sunday afternoons you'll be made to feel an instant couch potato upon seeing the teams of rowers sculling over the surface of the water in pond-skater fashion. The green space beyond the next car park offers an accessible riverside path, with hand-carved seating providing welcome stops. Longmarsh was once used by the local rifle volunteers, and you can still find the remains of the rifle butts at the far side of the strip of unusually (for south Devon) flat land.

The open space—once all saltmarsh—is a favourite with local families and dog walkers, and can be busy on Sunday afternoons. It is still a good space to admire the river as it flows away from the town, to walk in tall grass and be surrounded by clouds of butterflies in summer, and to pick blackberries in autumn.

2. A Walk around the Dartington Estate

In the 1920s, the American heiress Dorothy Whitney-Straight and her English husband, the agriculturalist Leonard Elmhirst, established a 'centre for experiments in rural reconstruction and progressive education' on a dilapidated estate bordering the River Dart at Dartington. Influenced by the progressive social ideas of Indian poet and thinker

Beside the Dart at Longmarsh

Rabindranath Tagore, and heeding his advice that they look for somewhere in Devon because of the softness of the landscape and gentleness
of climate, they bought the 800-acre mediæval estate, complete with deer
park, home farm and Great Hall. Over the next forty years they developed
a diverse community of artists, educationalists and agriculturalists with
two schools, innovative forestry and agricultural methods, a pottery, a
famous glassworks, a textile mill, a centre for the arts and an international summer school of music. Today, although much has changed, the
vision and philosophy of the original founders remain intact, and
continues to inform the many and diverse projects undertaken at Dartington. As a forestry man, Leonard Elmhirst was inclined to 'follow the
way the sap was flowing'. Now the sap flows in many different directions
on the estate. This can make the place rather hard to navigate, especially
for a visitor; there's always more to find out. It's part of the draw of the
place, as has been the case for the past seventy-five years.

For walking around the estate, the most popular path follows the
river. This may be picked up just beyond where the cycle path hangs a left
beside Berryman's Marsh. On the right, shortly after the second gate
posts (where the road narrows), are a gate and stile which lead into a field
beside the river. This path follows a riverside route through North Wood
to Huxham's Cross, where it is possible to pick up the public footpath,
which returns to the drive just beyond Dartington Lodge, via the Cider
Press and the cycle path.

A Riverside Walk

From Totnes it is possible to take a riverside walk or cycle to the Dartington estate. The path starts at the Old Bridge in Totnes on the town side
of the river, and eventually emerges on to the Dartington estate drive just
below the lodge entrance. From Borough Park this path is cycle-, buggy-
and wheelchair-friendly (radar keys for the gates along the path can be
hired from the Tourist Information Centre in the Town Mill, Totnes, just
beside the pedestrian exit from Safeway's car park). Either side of the
drive at this point are water meadows. These were once an arm of the
River Dart, with boats carrying their cargo as far up as The Queen's Arms
pub. Berryman's Marsh, on the river side of the drive, was set aside in
1991 to create a wetland habitat (attracting rare species of birds), wildflowers and grasses. It follows a route beside the water meadow along the
edge of the woodland to Shinner's Bridge, emerging at a cluster of workshops and shops around the **Cider Press Centre.**

After passing the old Tweed Mills and the two lime kilns for the estate, you will find **Dartington Pottery** on the right. Founded by Bernard Leach in the 1920s, it was here that he wrote *A Potter's Book*. Leach's involvement in Dartington lasted only five years, but his influence lives on, and the craft of pottery thrives. This is also due in part to the availability of good clay, for both ball and china clay are found in Devon.

Dart Pottery—as it is now known—produces the joyful and flamboyant designs of Janice Tchalenko. A hallmark of her work is that the designs cover all surfaces of the pot. Apple, Peacock, Orchid and Delphinium are the names of some of her bold designs, which are applied using sponges, brushes or slip trailers, giving a sense of immediacy and lightness of touch. Seconds are on sale at the Pottery shop for substantially less than the cost of a 'first'.

Further along the path is **Tridias**, which you enter at your peril, for this spacious, browsable toy shop holds a captivating range of toys and games, as well as an excellent book and tape section. The emphasis is on invention, from the potato clock to the spangly fairy outfit. The extensive 'hands on' Brio table serves to distract the children, allowing furtive purchases to be made. If you haven't the time to pause, pick up a catalogue and buy by mail order. **Tridias, Cider Press Centre, Dartington ☎ 01803 863957.**

Walking towards the main entrance of the Cider Press, you will find the **Book Shop**. It is worth dropping in here, if only for the idiosyncratic nature of the stock, which reflects both the community it comes from and the image it projects. Big on art and local interest, with lots of handsome books to browse through. **The Book Shop ☎ 01803 864171.**

Mind out for wandering jugglers as you cross the courtyard into the main Cider Press, which I shall deal with briefly as it is so well covered in mainstream guides, save to note one exhibit in the craft shop: the pottery of **Marianne De Trey**. Back in 1949 she took over the pottery at Dartington, and ran it for many years. Her pots are delicately understated, in porcelain and celadon. De Trey continues to work at Shinner's Bridge in the workshop built for David Leach all those years ago. **The Cider Press Centre, Dartington ☎ 01803 864171.**

Uphill from the plant shop and additional car parks, follow the footpath past Dartington cricket pitch to the left, and Foxhole to the right. This building once housed the famous progressive Dartington School, where pupils involved themselves in the small rural businesses of Dartington as part of their self-guided educational programme. William

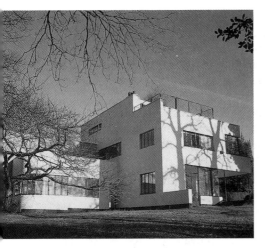

Curry, the first headmaster of the School and a passionate believer in modernism, was instrumental in employing the Swiss American architect William Lescaze to design **High Cross House**—the headmaster's house—a little further up the drive. Distinguished by brave blue walls and sharp geometric lines, it contrasts starkly with the soft grey stone of nearby buildings. Carefully restored over recent years, and furnished with pieces of its time and place, this 1932 international modernist house makes for an inspiring visit. Inside, amongst the rounded edges of the 1930s decor and furniture, are paintings and ceramics from the private collection which Dorothy and Leonard Elmhirst bequeathed to the Dartington Hall Estate. Concentrating upon the early part of the twentieth century, it comprises paintings (including Cecil Collins and Ben Nicholson) and ceramics (including Leach and Hamada).

The Dartington Hall Trust Archive is also held here, made up of letters, books (including private press books, typography and illustration that includes Eric Gill) photographs, films and tapes accumulated since 1925. Research and study groups may visit by appointment. Further examples of International Modernist style buildings to be found on the estate include those in Warren Lane, a particularly fine example being Warren House, which was built complete with dance floor, serpentine wall and sun-bathing balconies for the dancer Kurt Joos, who was resident there during the 1930s. **High Cross House, Dartington Hall ☎ 01803 864114.** Open from May to the end of October, Tuesday to Friday 2–4.30 pm. Entrance £2.50 (£1.50 concessions).

LUCCOMBE'S COFFIN

The original Luccombe oak was propagated in 1763 from a hybrid seedling which retained its leaves throughout the winter. At the age of around 70, William Luccombe had the tree cut down, and planks from it were stored under his bed. Thirty years later, when he eventually died at the age of 102, it was used to make his coffin.

High Cross House

Between High Cross House and Foxhole is the **Regional Centre for Organic Horticulture, Dartington.** Primarily a horticultural training centre, the organic produce grown here supplies the Dartington kitchens and local shops; any surplus is sold to the public. This can include vegetables, herbs, cut flowers, and all kinds of salads. Availability depends upon the season—it's a case of pot luck. **Regional Centre for Organic Horticulture ☎ 01803 867693.** Open 9.30 am–4 pm weekdays.

With Foxhole on your right, walk up to the junction with Dartington Drive. Turn left towards Dartington church. A couple of hundred yards down the road, take a right turn (signed SPARC and Craft Education Centre). South Devon Play and Resource Centre—also known as the scrapstore—is housed in The Old Chicken House at the end of the driveway. Inside, somewhere amongst rolls of coloured plastic sacks, fleece offcuts, reams of ribbons and sundry discards from local industry, can be found co-ordinators Ali Roscoe and Caroline Lakin. Join the scrapstore and you can fill a bag with chosen pieces for £1, as well as buy good quality art materials at low prices. The scrapstore brings in local artists to run all sorts of making workshops (felt making and patchwork caught my eye). There is also a stack of resources for hire: circus box, story bags, ball pool, batik box, multicultural resource boxes and badge making equipment, to name but a few. Upstairs there is a warm, light workshop which is available for hire, as well as a small exhibition space. Ring to check for opening hours. **SPARC, The Old Chicken House, Craft Education, Dartington ☎ 01803 847943.**

Around Dartington Hall

Under the archway, which is the entrance to the courtyard is the box office for **Dartington Arts**, where information can be gathered about what's on and bookings can be made for a wide range of events. **The Barn Theatre** is the home of film and small productions, while the mediaeval Great Hall provides an unusual venue for concerts and performances. Although a small place, Dartington has an international reputation for both mainstream and experimental arts, and attracts artists of a very high

> **TURKEY OAK**
>
> Between the College buildings at Lower Close and the entrance to the White Hart is a majestic turkey oak. Under the shade of this tree are planted hundreds of croci, which when in flower form a vast purple disc. Pilgrimages are made to see them and to say goodbye to winter.

ROBINS AT DARTINGTON

 Dartington Hall grounds are filled with birdlife and beautiful flowers. Ian Mercer, who was for many years chief officer of Dartmoor National Park, used to lead an annual common bird census in the grounds. The most common bird at Dartington is the robin, and it was here that some of the secrets of the robin's life were first discovered.

There was a young teacher, David Lack, teaching at Dartington Hall School. In 1934 he began a study of the robins living in the grounds. During four years he ringed 119 adults and 121 nestlings. To study their habits at close quarters he constructed two aviaries, both ten yards long, where the robins bred successfully. When the young were fledged, David Lack let them and their parents free.

In the autumn he found that about three-quarters of the females disappeared and did not return until the early spring. The males and the remaining quarter of the females stayed, having individual winter territories.

He listened to the song of the robin, and found that the spring song started in late December and continued until mid-June. He first heard the thinner, autumn song in late July, and this continued—a sad, weak reflection of the vigorous song of spring—until the spring song started again in December. In the autumn he discovered that not only the males sang: about half of the female robins were also singing.

Robins can live for about ten years, but David Lack revealed from ringing recoveries that average life expectancy is only just over a year. He pointed out that if there were no sparrowhawks, weasels, cats or disease, in ten years one pair would have multiplied to two million.

Robins use their red breasts for display, reinforcing the message of their song that this patch is theirs and intruders should go away. David Lack bought a tatty stuffed robin and placed it by some of the robins' nests, when they had young. The parents attacked it violently, in one case beheading the lifeless creature. He decided to develop the experiment, removing all of the parts of the bird until only a tuft of red breast feathers were left. Most of the robins still attacked the specimen. In contrast, when he painted over the breast of another stuffed robin with brown paint the Dartington robins took no notice.

calibre. Watch out too for free events, especially during the International Summer
School season (July–August), which is
awash with concerts and recitals. The
degree shows at the College of Arts (in
June) indicate the directions of contemporary arts and new media. **Dartington Arts
Box Office ☎ 01803 847070.**

Dartington Playgoers Each summer
the Dartington Playgoers put on a Shakespeare production in the gardens. There
are at least one or two other Playgoers'
productions per season, and these (more
than the weather) are reliably good. Make
a summer's evening of it: walk up to
Dartington, and take a light supper at
The White Hart—the restaurant and pub in the courtyard, to the left of
the entrance to the Great Hall. This can be followed by a walk in the
gardens before catching a film or a show. And if the walk back seems all
too much, call a taxi.

Dartington Hall Gardens Below The Gallery and to the right is the
arched entrance to the courtyard—with the Barn Theatre on the left
inside the archway. Take the path across the courtyard and past The
White Hart into the gardens.

Dorothy Elmhirst absorbed herself in the making of this 'English
Garden' for over 40 years, involving amongst others the American landscape gardener Beatrix Farrand. Trees in the gardens are particularly

remarkable, with many of the finest
dating from the nineteenth century,
and Spanish chestnuts above the
terraces are thought to be from the
mid-sixteenth century. The Luccombe
oaks, of which there are two, are
thought to be from the original
planting by the Exeter nurseryman
William Luccombe.

Numerous paths have been carved
through the gardens, moving from
formal to informal planting. Each

Dartington Hall Gardens: church tower and summer house

season brings something special. In winter the skeleton of the garden is exposed, and vistas are cleared. In spring, the magnolias and camellias come into their own (the Camellia Walk was one of Beatrice Ferrand's contributions to the garden). In summer, the demonstrative herbaceous border mixes soft yellows, mauves and blues in a pattern which repeats itself every second wall column. In autumn the foliage is a riot of pinks, yellows, oranges and reds. Children love the space of the gardens—one of the thatched huts now used by the gardeners was built as a Wendy house for the young Elmhirst children. Kids have a ball leaping up and down flights of steps, making entrances from behind the clipped hedge wings of the open air theatre in the Tiltyard, and discovering dens and secret pathways. Sadly, the temptation to roly-poly down the terraces above the Tiltyard must be resisted. The Dartington Hall Gardens are open daily. Suggested donation £2.00. A *Guide to the Gardens* (by Reginald Snell) is available at Reception, under the arch in the entrance to the courtyard.

DARTINGTON YOUTH HOSTEL

If the acronym YHA fills you with visions of toil lists, emptying latrines and single sex dorms with lights out by 9.30, then take a look at the Dartington Youth Hostel. This sixteenth-century cottage and annexe stands beside Bidwell Brook in an idyllic hamlet close to Dartington. It makes an ideal base from which to explore the locality. Inexpensive accommodation is in five- or six-bedded rooms, and family rooms can be booked if available. In winter, when the hostel is closed, it is possible to book the whole place—ideal for those extended family 'do's', or for getting together with a bunch of friends on neutral territory. **Dartington Youth Hostel, Lownyard, Dartington, Totnes ☎ 01803 862303**.

Dartington Hall Gardens: swan fountain by Willi Soukop

Annual Events to Note

Ways With Words A literary fortnight in early summer (usually July) with a surfeit of workshops, talks, readings, and lunches, drawing the literati together at Dartington. Kay Dunbar, the local organiser of this festival, brings together both crowd-pulling names and more marginal speakers. Ways With Words also organise reading and writing 'At Home' days throughout the winter. **Ways With Words, Droridge Farm ☎ 01803 867311.**

Riverford Farm Pumpkin Day   One day a year, towards the end of October, Riverford Organic Vegetables have a Pumpkin Day at Wash Farm, Staverton. Pumpkins mark the route so you don't get lost in the lanes. Visitors get a bumpy trailer ride around the farm, and a talk about how it all works. Then it's back to a shed heaving with pumpkins, and piping hot soup. A great family outing. Proceeds go to Oxfam. **Riverford Organic Vegetables, Wash Barn, Buckfastleigh ☎ 01803 762720.**

A Gentle Walk to Staverton

A little further upriver from Dartington is Staverton. This short circular walk, starting at Staverton station, can be reached by train from Totnes or Buckfastleigh.

Alight from the steam train at Staverton station (or pay 50p to park in the station car park across the road) and take a left just before the road bridge. Walk past some disused workshops, and you will find yourself at the start of a delightful child-friendly riverside walk. The route follows a path between the railway line and the River Dart. The walk is perfect for small children, with shady riverside beaches beside shallow waters. A

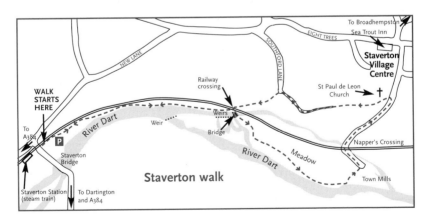

little further on is an island, which may involve wet feet as the depth of water to be forded reaches around wellie height. Once on the island it is an ideal spot for picnics, den making and tree climbing.

I walked this route with friends, their two-year-old daughter, and buggy. The only tricky bit was crossing the sluice gate beside the weir. It was early February, and the woodland floor was white with snowdrops. The path emerges at the mill then crosses the railway at Napper's Cross. Follow the path up into the village. At the church of St. Paul de Leon, walkers can choose to continue the circular walk or head up into the village for a stop at the Sea Trout Inn for refreshment. The return route is easy to follow down through the churchyard to the gate, along the path with meadow to the right, and onto a stretch of minor road. Take a left left after Sweet William Cottage, and after the path crosses the railway rejoins the riverside route back to the station. The walk is around two miles in all.

Riverford Organic Vegetables have their headquarters at Wash Barn in Staverton. Tours of the organic farm are held most weekends, starting at 11 am with a guided walk around the fields, and a chance to gather fruits and vegetables in season before a bumpy tractor and trailer ride. At the end of the tour people spill into the spanking new field kitchen for a specially prepared lunch and an opportunity to taste the vegetables the have just seen growing. Chef Jane Baxter, who trained at the River Café, has a way of surprising and delighting the palette, and her plum and almond tart and hazelnut pavlova with raspberries are exquisite. Saturday tours are free for box customers, and lunch is around £12.00 for adults and £6 for children. Lots of other events are planned at the field kitchen: organic children's parties with treasure hunts in the polytunnels and running through the maize fields, school visits, cookery demonstrations . . . best to visit the website: **www.riverford.co.uk** ☎ **01803 762721.**

Just off the A384 Buckfastleigh–Totnes Road is **Riverford Farm Shop**. This is a one-stop shop, with fresh-picked organic vegetables, unforgettable pork sausages, bacon from the farm, cheese galore, local mussels, oysters, moreish olives and the best chocolate. Lots more information on the website **www.riverfordfarmshop** ☎ **01803 762523.**

Riverford Farm Tour at Wash Barn, Staverton

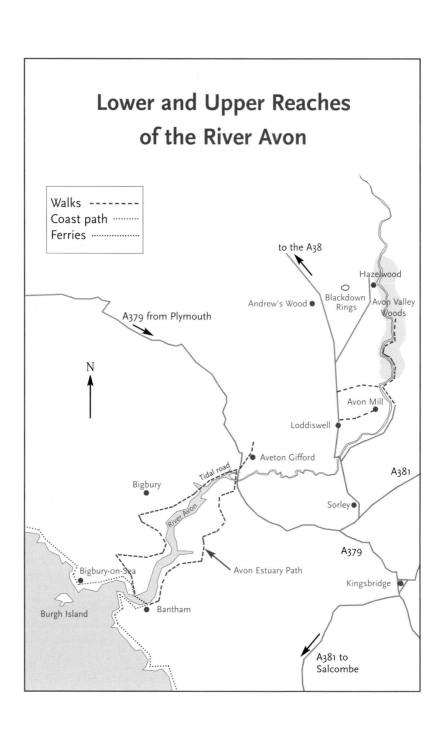

Lower and Upper Reaches
of the River Avon

Walks -------
Coast path ·········
Ferries ················

to the A38

Hazelwood

Andrew's Wood ●   Blackdown
Rings

Avon Valley
Woods

A379 from Plymouth

N

Avon Mill

Loddiswell ●

Aveton Gifford ●

A381

Bigbury
●

Tidal road

Sorley ●

River Avon

A379

Bigbury-on-Sea

Avon Estuary Path

Kingsbridge ●

Burgh Island

Bantham

A381 to
Salcombe

Chapter 4—Avon Valley

Beginning in Bantham, this chapter covers two separate stretches of the River Avon. The first is a walk around the stretch of tidal estuary, from the ferry crossing point at Bantham, up to Aveton Gifford and back along the east bank of the estuary to Bantham. The second stretch starts with Blackdown Rings and Andrew's Wood (Stanton Moor), then moves to the Hazelwood Estate, the village of Loddiswell, and a walk in the higher Avon Valley.

The River Avon keeps a low profile, as south Devon rivers go. It remains relatively unspoilt and undeveloped, for sandy banks at the river mouth prevent its use by all but small craft. Because of this, the Avon Estuary has resisted the 'boaty' image of its neighbours, the Kingsbridge and Salcombe Estuary and the Dart. Instead it offers long stretches of peaceful riverside walks through exceptional countryside packed with wildlife.

We first explore the area south of Loddiswell—the lower reaches— with its broad valley which progresses gently through marshland, on through woodland and several dispersed farmsteads, to the sea.

The Lower Reaches

Bantham Bantham has a wide expanse of sandy bay where the waves break far enough out to make it one of the few surfing beaches around. Kite enthusiasts meet here regularly to take advantage of the strong winds which can batter this part of the coast. On gentler days, it can be

Bantham beach

PLANTS AROUND BANTHAM

The grass that flourishes in the sand dunes at Bantham is a remarkable plant. It is called marram grass, and only really thrives in moving sand. It brings about its own destruction, for the vast underground network of roots it pushes out through moving sand consolidate it, so that it no longer moves. As the tall tussocks above ground grow, they provide a place where other plants may become established. The arching leaves of the marram are grooved so that they can curve round in the heat of the day, closing up like a drainpipe, keeping moisture from evaporating. I love watching, early in the morning, drops of dew dripping off the tips of the marram grass leaves and making tiny crater like depressions in the sand.

Inland from the sand dunes, where the marram is dying and other grasses are taking over, you can find large patches of iris. This is stinking iris, which is most at home on chalky soil. In summer, it has beautifully veined purple flowers; they look wonderful but smell horrid. In autumn, the big seed-pods open to reveal lots of orange berries, which to someone's eyes must have resembled underdone meat for another name for it is 'roast beef plant'.

If you search diligently you may find the pale pink pyramids of the pyramidal orchid. In June and early July it grows among the fine grasses. I first found it growing on the chalk downs of Kent, but it is equally at home at Bantham and Bigbury.

Bantham is also a paradise for butterflies. Look out for the black and white marbled whites, the blues, the browns, and the migrant painted ladies. Also the six-spot burnet, a day-flying moth which lays its eggs on the 'eggs and bacon' flowers of bird's-foot-trefoil. Look out for the green and black chequered caterpillars nibbling the leaves or climbing a stem to make its cocoon, like a vertical golden hammock. The moths zoom about on sunny days. It is only when they are still resting upon yellow ragwort blossom or purple knapweed, sipping nectar through their long black tongues, that their black wings, seared with scarlet lines and spots, are visible.

perfect for a trip to the beach with the kids, the sand being ideal for castles, and the sea for swimming, where it is designated safe. The beach is reached by a single track road which passes through the pretty village of Bantham. Sadly this is all too often obscured by a scrum of traffic on a summer's day. It has, amongst other things, a good pub—**The Sloop Inn**, which sells real ales and local cider, and whose restaurant specialises in seafood dishes.

The useful village shop doubles as a café, with tables on a terrace which overlooks the estuary. **The Sloop Inn, Bantham ☎ 01548 560215.**

The sand dunes of Bantham support all kinds of wildlife. The marram grass which tops the dunes is the plant that holds the dunes in place, and between the clumps grow a wealth of salt-tolerant plants. These include sea bindweed, sand sedge, and a bright yellow green moss (*Tortula ruraliformis*). Also found in the sandy hollows are two poisonous plants, the Woody Nightshade and rare Henbane. At night, watch out for glow worms: the ham is home to the rare species *lampyrus noctilica*. Peppered around the dunes are also the tiny shells of dune snails, the pretty white spire-shaped shells with ginger markings (*Cochlicella acuta*) as described by Kingsbridge naturalist George Montague.

'Ham' being saxon for settlement, it is probable that Bantham Ham was an ancient settlement. It was the great storm of 1703 which first uncovered evidence of this when hurricane winds and giant waves washed away the dunes. Artefacts found on the site since include fish hooks, pottery, bone tools and javelin heads. These have been dated between Iron Age and mediaeval periods. Many finds from this period made by Ann Jenkins of East Buckland can been seen in Torquay Museum.

Sticks It is worth noting, particularly if a long walk is about to be taken, that the stick-maker Henry Alexander lives in the village. He first learned the technique as a boy scout, and 51 years on he makes walking sticks from a variety of local woods (hazel, ash, blackthorn, sweet chestnut, holly, gorse)—some twisted by honeysuckle, and burrs forming the handles of others. Wonderful objects, and functional to boot—essential equipment for walking the hills of South Devon. Visit by appointment. **Henry Alexander ☎ 01548 561182.**

The Sloop Inn at Bantham

MATT'S GUIDE TO SURFING
IN THE SOUTH HAMS

Matt Burner is 15 years old, and has been surfing since he was 7. In September 2004, he finished 2nd at the British Nationals, at under 14 level. In Spring 2005 he was invited to join the English Surf squad.

How to get started

So you want to surf in the South Hams? Well, there's a lot you need to know to keep yourself safe and to have a good time. Before you start, you do need to be a fairly good swimmer; most surf schools insist you can swim a minimum of fifty metres and feel confident in breaking waves. You also need a dedicated/slightly loopy family who will follow you to the ends of the earth in search of that elusive, perfect wave. The best way to get going, if you're a novice, is to approach a local surf school. We are really lucky to have **Discovery Surf School** based nearby, and run by the nationally renowned surfer Martin Connolly. He holds all the British Surf Association (BSA) qualifications and public liability insurance. He will supply all the kit, except swimsuits and towels! With beginners, Martin operates a ratio of one coach to six surfers, so you will get a lot attention and support. If you do want to buy your own kit the best place to go to is Plymouth: there are quite a few good quality surf shops there and the assistants are very helpful. **Discovery Surf School ☎ 07813 639622 www.discoverysurf.com.**

What you need

A good long board . . . don't try to learn on a three-fin short board! The ideal learner board is a spongy swell board. They are long, wide and very buoyant. They are also soft, so don't hurt so much if they hit you! If you're not sure whether stand up is the style for you, you might like to try body boarding: the boards are sold in all the good surf shops and the assistants will help with sizes and tail shapes.

Get a good, close fitting wet suit, as too many baggy areas just fill with cold water and won't keep you warm. You may also need boots, gloves and helmet if you plan to surf all year round. A rash vest under the wetsuit will help stop painful rubbed areas of skin under the arms and other delicate areas!

Where to go

I'm not going to give away my secret spots, but there a lot of well known local beaches. Bantham has the most consistent breaking wave on the south coast and is popular with surfers of all standards. It is situated at the mouth of the River Avon, just down from Aveton Gifford. Next door (travelling west) you'll find Bigbury-on-Sea. This is another large open sandy beach offering plenty of variation for the more novice surfer. When conditions are difficult or there are no waves, we travel north to the coast of Devon and Cornwall, but you will need to get a good map and have access to the internet to gather the necessary information to stop you making a wasted journey.

Daily Surf forecasts can be found on many internet sites: one of the best is **www.a1surf.com**. On there you will find SJ's forecast or Soul Searcher—both will give you good local information. **www.bbc.co.uk/weather/coast/tides/southwest** is the best place to find the most up-to-date tidal information for just about any southwest venue you can think of, **BUT DO TAKE NOTE** of all the comments supplied on these sites. Experienced surfers have provided the information and will certainly know if beginners should be in the sea and surfing. Even if there aren't any warning notes, you are the best judge of your ability—don't go in if you have any doubts, and never surf alone!

I hope you enjoy your surfing and find this information helpful. Maybe I'll see you sometime . . .

Photo © Ray Chuss, Talltrees Photography

Matt Burner in action

The Avon Estuary Walk

The River Avon rises on Dartmoor and flows twenty-two miles to the sea. Half a mile above Aveton Gifford Bridge there is a weir which marks the upper limit of the tides in the Avon Estuary. For the next four miles the river flows through a narrow, steep-sided valley to the sea where it empties into Bigbury Bay. The inlet almost dries at low tide, except for the shallow river channel. It is the most sandy of any of the South Hams estuaries, the last two miles having broad shoals of sand.

Small colonies of seabird breed within the inlet and it is used for over wintering by the common sandpiper, little egrets and greenshanks. The inlet is a nursery for sea bass and Atlantic salmon. Sea trout migrate to the inlet to spawn upriver.

The Route

This is a nine-mile waymarked circular route, from Bantham Quay, crossing the water by ferry (between Easter and September) to the north bank at Cockleridge, via Bigbury and Aveton Gifford, where the bridge is crossed back onto the south bank and back to Bantham. The route is waymarked by yellow arrows and blue 'Avon Estuary Walk' signs with a heron logo.

Walkers should note that there are low- and high-tide routes from Bigbury-on-Sea, and to Aveton Gifford from North Efford. Here the high-tide route is over a mile longer than the low-tide route. Ferry crossings from Bantham are booked through Harbour Master and Ferryman **Neil Schroeter 01548 561196 (day)** or **01548 550983 (evenings).**

From Bantham Car Park

From Bantham car park, head towards the village. Take the turning left down to Bantham Quay. The ferry departs to Cockleridge from the small hard at the water's edge.

The thatched boathouse beside the Quay was built in 1937 to commemorate the accession of King George VI. Figureheads support

The east bank of the Avon at Bantham

two corners of the building, one representing
Lady Franklin. This came from the
missionary ship 'Frankfort', which she had
built in memory of her husband Sir John
Franklin who died in 1847 whilst searching
for the North West Passage.

When crossing the estuary, look back
towards Bantham Quay. Along the waterfront to the left of the Quay stands an
unusually tall building. This was once a
pilchard cellar, built in 1779 when the pilchard industry thrived in
Bigbury Bay, forming the basis of the local economy.

From Bigbury-on-Sea

Low-tide route *If the tide is low it is possible to walk along the beach to Cockleridge Ham. From the Car Park go down the steps beach beside the Venus
Café and continue left along the beach to Cockleridge where there is a concrete
slipway. Join the coastal path to the Cockleridge Ferry. The Avon Estuary Walk
is way marked from this point.*

High-tide route *Turn right coming out of the car park onto the road. Cross
the access road to beach, and follow the coast path route onto Clematon Hill,*

THE PILCHARD INDUSTRY

'Huers' or look-outs posted at high places along the coast would alert fishermen with
a 'hue and cry' when an approaching shoal of pilchards was sighted. Within minutes
of the huers' cry, small boats were launched into the estuary and out to sea to the
west side of the island (for the tide was too strong on the other). From here, the seine
nets were shot. Astounding numbers were caught in a single haul. In August 1810
one net was recorded as having taken a thousand hogshead. With two thousand
fishes to a hogshead, this amounted to two million pilchards. It is no surprise that
pilchard numbers were dwindling by the 1860s and the industry was in decline.

'When Pilchards are received at the factory, they are neither beheaded nor
emboweled but are piled in regular heaps lying upon each other with their heads
outwards, being sprinkled with coarse bay salt between each layer. After a certain
time they are compressed to extract the oil for use'. (Colonel Montague,1808)

With pilchards thrown over the land for manure and their oil used to light
the village, Bantham in the 1800s must have been a very smelly place!

Boats at Bantham

past the cliff top houses and onto the main road (Folly Hill). Turn right at
Public Footpath sign after Mount Folly Farm. Walk alongside the field
boundary, cross the stile onto the Golf Course, where the Avon Estuary Walk
route is re-joined.

Cockleridge

Scattered all about the sand in Cockleridge are cockle shells, and locals
are occasionally seen gathering them for the pot. Watch out for notices
advising the public not to eat the cockles. These appear occasionally
when toxic algae is present in the river.

The calcium in snail shells, shell fragments and rabbit bones
produces a sandy soil suitable for plants which grow on chalk or limestone: ladies' bedstraw, pyramidal orchids and wild clematis are some of
the 80 different plant types to be found here. Also watch out for Burnet
moths and the white and black marbled white butterfly.

From the Quay in Cockleridge, head toward the steep earth steps cut into
the hillside. The route is waymarked by the Heron sign as well as 'Public Foot-
path to Bigbury'. Cross over the stile and keep to the right side of the field. At
the top of the field turn left along the boundary, then turn right into the Golf
Course road. The observation post is a good place to pause for breath.
From the top there is a sweeping view of Bigbury Bay, Burgh Island, and
on the skyline to the east is the distinctive spire of Malborough Church.
Continue up the road, then down the hill to the Green Keeper's Nissen
Hut. Turn right through the gate to Hexdown Farm. Having passed
through two gates, descend towards the water. The landscaped gardens
of Villa Crusoe lie at the bottom of the hill.

Villa Crusoe

This 1934 Italianate villa is so named because it has in its living room a
plain brick-built fireplace with brick hearth and wooden mantle. The fireplace once belonged in 16 St James's Square in Bristol, and it was in front
of this fireplace that the writer Daniel Defoe is said to have first heard the
story of Alexander Selkirk ('Robinson Crusoe') around the mid 1600s.
How or why it ended up in Villa Crusoe is uncertain. But there it is.

The waymarker directs the walker into a shady, tree-lined avenue.
This is a time to enjoy the remoteness of the Avon valley, and in springtime to watch out for dog violets, or the perfumed sweet violet.

Devon Violets The violet has long been associated with Devon—the
first violet farm was established at Dawlish in 1916. The steady growth in

the industry was encouraged by the introduction of a tariff on imported flowers, and violet growing increased by 500 percent in Dawlish alone. Mr and Mrs George Zambra of The Windward Violet Farm in Dawlish planted between 7,000 and 10,000 'Princesse de Galles' plants annually, and introduced seven cultivars into circulation—'Pamela Zambra', 'Windward' and 'Mrs R Barton' being three of them. Mrs Zambra also produced perfume, crystallized violets and a violet–flavoured honey.

Follow the sign to the permissive footpath which runs through the field alongside the main road. Pass through a gate into a second field. A waymarker signs a public footpath to Bigbury Village—an opportunity to wander round the village or find refreshment at the Royal Oak pub. Otherwise continue along the route following the sign to Milburn Orchard.

Crossing the field towards Doctor's Wood, the church of St Mary the Virgin at Churchstow may be visible on the skyline. Cross the stile into the wood.

Emerging from the woods, the path continues across an open field along the fence posts to a stile which leads into the first of two steeply sloping fields. Aveton Gifford is now visible in the distance, and below are the salt marshes.

Saltmarshes

Growing in the saltmarshes along the Avon are plants such as glasswort, spartina and sea purslane. Glasswort, otherwise known as marsh samphire, is a popular wild food in season.

Walk down the hill towards Milburn Orchard, cross the stile and head for the foreshore.

The path passes briefly through the grounds of The Oratory, a private house which stands upon the site of a 14th-century oratory dedicated to St Milburga, who founded a monastery at Wenlock in Shropshire around AD 690. As well as healing the sick, she had the power to communicate with birds, and was said to help farmers by charming their scarecrows. It was also recorded that she prevented a flock of wild geese from doing damage to crops. Years later, pilgrims to her tomb purchased little leaden geese as mementos. A statue of her, with dove in hand, can be seen in the grounds close to the entrance gates of The Oratory.

Here the route joins the tidal road, which is impassable for about two hours either side

Washing samphire in the sea

THE BUSH CRICKET

After walking southwards down the length of the tidal road, search among the saltmarsh vegetation beyond the little car park: you may see coneheads leaping from leaf to leaf on the tall green club rushes. These are a type of bush cricket, a little insect like a grasshopper but with over-long antennae and orange eyes on stalks. Their green and black bodies are long and slender, and the female has an ovipositor—a sword with which to lay eggs—curving from her back end.

of high tide. Turn left here if tempted by the lure of seafood.

The Oyster Shack is about 200 yards up the road on the right hand side. Here tables and chairs are set out under a vine- and honeysuckle-shaded canopy, where delicious seafood is served. This unlicensed eating place (don't forget to bring your own wine) is the stuff of gorgeous lazy lunches, where, because the food is so fresh and delicious, one wants to try everything. It's a busy place, so book in advance. **The Oyster Shack ☎ 01548 810876** (ring for opening times).

At Low Tide follow the waymarked tidal route to the right which takes the walker to Aveton Gifford Bridge.

At High Tide follow the yellow arrow attached to the public footpath marker across the road—a longer route of 2.5 miles. After the stepping stones, the route follows a path above the creek. At the head of the creek (at Duke's Mill) are the cut stumps of pollarded willows which were harvested for many years for basketmaking, which took place in the stone building standing close by the packhorse bridge.

The Woodmason Family

The name Woodmason in Aveton Gifford can be traced back over 600 years, and for 300 years the family worked as basket makers. They lived at Duke's Mill where they grew willows on plots beside the basket maker's hut. James Woodmason, who died in 1965, made fishing baskets, and 'mauns'—round baskets used by farmers for carrying mangolds, potatoes and other farm produce. The cut willow was stacked in the stream until the stakes could be stripped of their bark, and the willows were dried in the sun to whiten. In this part of Devon willows were never referred to as 'withies' but always 'willows'.

After crossing the packhorse bridge, continue uphill along the road. Turn right into Drunkard's Hill. At the top of the hill cross over the stile to the right, and head for a second stile to the left. Keep to the right hand boundary of the steeply sloping field. At the bottom cross the stile and descend steps. Turn left into the minor road. At Skipper's Hill Cottage take a sharp right and continue up the hill to the main road. Turn right onto the path parallel to the main road, pass under the road via the subway and turn left into Timbers Car Park.

Here is an opportunity to explore the village of Aveton Gifford. For those wishing to do so in detail, an informative self-guided walk pointing out historic landmarks of interest is available from local TICs and from the Fisherman's Rest pub.

Crossing the Water

"At Aveton Gifford . . . the River Avon, or Aune was seen winding through a wide vale the pasturage of which had a marshy look and across the whole width of which had been thrown a bridge." (Rev. John Swete, *Travels in Georgian Devon*, 1879–1900)

A ford useable at low-tide probably existed between South and North Efford (ebb ford) before the bridge was completed around 1440. The 1200–metre causeway is supported by 6 arches, one of which is over dry land. It was widened by village stonemason Walter Macey in 1817, using stone quarried from the site of the houses to the east side of the road at Bridge End. Aveton Gifford is sometimes referred to as the village of masons, and has long ties with the building industry. This was probably built upon the barge trade in the estuary when stone, limestone, sand timber and other building materials were landed at Bridge End Quay.

Cross the bridge to the south bank of the river, and turn right towards South Efford House. Carry on up to the top of the hill, where the track meets a private road. Turn right on to the road to Stadbury Manor and Farmhouse, which was first recorded in the Domesday Book in 1086. Turn left into a green lane. Turn right at the field gateway. Before a second gate, bear left down the hill. Follow path down to Stiddicombe Creek.

Stiddicombe Creek

A good place to pause or even picnic, Stiddicombe Creek is a natural adventure playground, with a beach, and a collection of springy grass tussocks with water running between them (ideal for long jump practice, with a touch of danger beneath). On the north side of the finger of the creek is a lime kiln, much favoured by the people of Bantham as a picnic spot.

Cross the rope bridge, and climb steps. Follow the waymarked lower path through the gate into Stiddicombe Woods.

Stiddicombe Woods was planted around a hundred years ago. It suffered badly from storms in 1990, the casualties from which lie in the water below, swathed with seaweed. There still remains in the wood a fine collection of sweet chestnut trees.

Leaving the woods through the gate at the top left-hand corner, the landscape opens up to a sweeping view down the estuary to Bigbury Bay. The path lies above a broad sandy stretch of the Avon. Across on the west bank, to the right of Villa Crusoe is Hexdown Quay. Upstream from here are the oyster beds.

Oyster Beds

In Roman times, native oysters would have been plentiful in the deeper waters of the Avon estuary, but over the centuries oysters were overfished and had almost disappeared by the end of the industrial revolution. Moves are afoot to reintroduce the native oyster into Devon waters. The species farmed along the Avon is the Pacific Oyster (*Crassostrea gigas*). Not being a native species, it is unable to spawn naturally and has to be introduced into the water in net bags when about the size of a thumbnail. The nets are then attached to table-like steel racks; 18–24 months later they are ready for harvesting. The oysters undergo a 42-hour cleaning process before being sold for consumption. Mussels are also farmed in these waters.

This is now the final leg to Bantham. The path curves to the left. Go through the gate and follow the track. Cross the stream and climb over the stile and up the steps. Negotiate the narrow opening (not for the broad beamed) and turn right. The next gate takes the walker into the residential part of Bantham. Turn right at the main road and head back to Bantham Ham.

Upper Reaches of the Avon Valley

In this second section of the Avon, we explore an area north of Loddiswell where the river

Figurehead on thatched house at Bantham

flows fast through the narrow steep-sided valley, through dense woodland and lush flora. There is no convenient network of public footpaths
to link the areas covered here, partly because of issues of land ownership,
but also because some areas are very sensitive as they support rare
wildlife species. Because of the special nature of this area, we shall treat
this section as a series of discrete places.

1.Blackdown Rings and Andrew's Wood

The Avon flows southward, past Topsham Bridge and through the steep
wooded valleys now under the guardianship of the Woodland Trust. On
the heights either side of the valley stand the Iron Age hill forts of Stan-
borough and Blackdown Rings.

On occasions, it's a relief to climb up to such heights, above the
shadow and shelter of the hills, to get a larger sense of the South Hams.
At six hundred and forty feet above sea level, **Blackdown Rings**, a couple
of miles north of Loddiswell, is just such a place. At this exposed and
ancient site, which is studded with wind-battered oaks and blackthorn, a
helpful directional map identifies landmarks round 360 degrees, with
Dartmoor to the north, Totnes to the north-east, Dartmouth to the east
and Start Bay to the south-west. Blackdown Rings takes its name from
the vast earthworks which encircle the hilltop, an Iron Age fort which
was built around 400 BC. The earthworks are still visible, as is the motte
and bailey castle constructed by the Normans after the conquest in 1066.
Rabbits now burrow in the Iron Age embankment, and 'sausage lichens'
blow in the wind from the gnarled oak trees growing in the Iron Age
ditch. Blackdown was one of the last areas of the South Hams to become
cultivated, remaining as heathland until quite recently. Lead was mined
here for a short time in the nineteenth century, but the site has been left
unexcavated. Once a part of the Hazelwood estate, it is now owned by the
Arundell Charity, which was founded in 1591 by Sir Matthew Arundell

ANDREW'S WOOD

Only half a mile's walk away from Blackdown Rings is Andrew's Wood, or Stanton Moor as it used to be known. Stanton Moor was a group of fields—mostly rough pasture—with a small farm at the southern end. In the middle of the nineteenth century the farm fell into disuse, and some of the wet fields were invaded by seedlings from the mature trees on the hedgebanks. Birch and pussy willow came first, oak slowly followed, and after half a century it was shading out the short-lived birch. As the century progressed, more fields fell into disuse. It was here at Stanton Moor that Reverend Keble Martin and other botanists found the heath lobelia in the 1890s. It was a rare plant then, and now it only grows on six sites in Britain. In the 1960s Col. and Mrs Walker owned Stanton Moor, and the neighbouring farm and house of Woolston. Their son Andrew, who loved the woodland and old pasture fields, was killed in a road accident while serving in the army. Upon leaving the area shortly after his death, Andrew's parents sold Stanton Moor to the Devon Wildlife Trust, on condition that it should from now on be known as Andrew's Wood, in memory of their son.

The purple-blue spikes of the heath lobelia are to be seen at their best in bloom during July and August, growing up to 2 ft 6 inches high in clearings around the wood. Also found in the clearings are the rare ragged-robin, heath spotted and marsh orchids, yellow bartsia, devil's-bit scabious and royal fern. The tufted grasses and rushes are equally important. Willow warblers and tree pipits, migrants from Africa, nest in tussocks. Adders and lizards bask on the warm quartzite boulders. In early spring, the brimstone butterfly is one of the first to emerge. Then in midsummer the silver-washed fritillaries (our largest butterfly) emerge, their orange upper wings delicately lined with black, the underwings rippled with waves of silver. Resting on the woodland paths can be seen the speckled wood butterfly.

In winter, the tussocks that shelter birds nests in summer now provide extra insulation for the hibernating dormice in their winter nests. They are snugly rolled up inside thick balls of grass.

'for the good and behoof of parishioners of Loddiswell'. This landmark is
a site to bring a kite to on a clear blue
day and get blown all over the place. A
leaflet about Blackdown Rings is available at the Tourist Information Centre
in Kingsbridge.

Andrew's Wood isn't signed on the
main road. The discreet car park is a
turning to the left off the road beyond
MGM Nurseries and before Blackdown
Rings. There are two marked routes through this remarkable woodland,
both well within the capacities of small children: the 'Frog' route is the
shorter, and the 'Ant' route slightly longer. Both move between woods and
clearings on well constructed walkways, bridges and stepping stones. The
detailed guide book fleshes out the walks with fascinating information
about some of the things which can be seen in the different seasons.
Should you wish for a guided walk or even a 'nature watch' in Andrew's
Wood, they are sometimes included in the calendars of events produced
by Devon Wildlife Trust and the South Devon AONB events programme.
A Guide to Andrew's Wood by Gordon Waterhouse is on sale at Loddiswell Village shop, or at the Tourist Information Centre in Kingsbridge.

2. Hazelwood Estate

It was the draw of the extraordinary
Avon valley which brought a group of
women together to purchase sixty-four
acres of the Hazelwood Estate in 1989.
They would shudder to be called a
community; rather a bunch of individuals thrown together, who have
invented this unique centre. The house
itself takes guests and runs courses,
alongside a programme of music and
esoteric events. In addition there are
four self-catering cottages on the steeply
sloping valley which tumbles down to
the River Avon. The co-owners of **Hazelwood House** are also involved with an

international peace initiative, and have hosted refugees from many parts of the world. Coincidentally the Quaker founder of the estate, Richard Peake, directed his energies and wealth from the tea trade towards the spread of peace principles. He financed the building of the churches in Loddiswell and Ugborough, as well as supporting less well-heeled Tory candidates. The financing of the current Hazelwood project has been a struggle, and the upkeep of the elderly buildings quite a challenge. Opportunities exist for volunteers to work on the estate, planting, renovating, or scrub clearing. Contact Hazelwood House for more details. Gold, silver, and pure spring water (bottled at source—ideal for babies—and available at the house) have all been discovered around Hazelwood. An elderly pollarded oak stands beside the entrance to the house. Inside, the dimly lit hall, smelling of wood smoke, leads into a series of homely rooms, well worn and relaxed.

Hazelwood would be the ideal place to retreat in midwinter for books, walks and reflection, or to take tea and a walk beside the Avon.

For a programme of events and details of accommodation, contact Hazelwood Estate, Loddiswell, Kingsbridge ☎ 01548 821232.

3. Loddiswell

Loddiswell village—or Lodda's well, three hundred feet above sea level, has one of the few village greens in the South Hams. In 1850 Loddiswell was listed as having three mills, four tailors, one woolcomber, cattle and pigs (providing leather for the boot-maker), a blacksmith, a wheelwright and three inns. A family called Luscombe manufactured yellow ochre, which was found in local clay deposits, in Loddiswell.

With the bounds of this parish enclosing some of the most stunning scenery in the South Hams, it is no wonder that Loddiswell preserves its independence. It still supports a number of small businesses, of which I will mention just a few.

Heron Valley Cider This fine cider is made nearby and can be bought in the village shop along with Steve Bradley's exceptional apple and refreshing grapefruit and apple juice.

Ham Farm Peet Leather designs sumptuous hats, coats and wall pieces: sculptural forms in felts saturated with royal colours. Carl Hahn makes

Hazelwood boathouse

unique, complex pieces of furniture. **Ring for an appointment ☎ 01548 550861.**

Cherry Cherry There is something of the boarding school girls together atmosphere in this tiny pinkly lit and flowery front room in Loddiswell which is home to Cherry Cherry. Certainly not a shop for the sartorially fainthearted: rails are filled with designer clothes imported from New Zealand, Australia and Paris that are fashioned from fabrics so delicate you could blow them away. Pretty lace, silk, satin and net are gathered, ruched, tapered and slit into all manner of skirts, tops and dresses which can be layered any which way. Take tea in delicate china, dress up, waft a little then sparkle a bit— the jewellery from Paris and New Zealand is exquisite. If a little at sea, seek guidance from owner and discerning stylist Sally Ann. **Cherry Cherry, open Saturdays 10.00–4.00 or by appointment. 1 The Bank, Fore Street, Loddiswell ☎ 01548 550530.**

MGM Nurseries This family-run nursery specialises in trees and shrubs, and grows a range of herbaceous plants, alpines and heathers. They also stock a selection of more exotic plants such as olive and citrus trees, palms and bamboos. Liz and Malcolm Montague's smallholding with chickens, Soay sheep, goats, other small animals and all sorts of birds will be sure to divert non-gardeners, while those with 'the bug' get down to the serious business of plant buying. **MGM Nurseries, Woolston Lodge, Loddiswell ☎ 01548 550754.**

ADDENDUM

Fifty-one deaths were recorded in and around Loddiswell in 1590 between 16th March and 12th September. A number of the victims were registered as coming from and around Stanton Moor. Afterwards, locals regarded the moor as an unhealthy spot. One Loddiswell woman remembered being told when she was a girl in the late 1800s not to go there for fear of disease. It followed that the heath was let alone, it seems, for centuries. Perhaps this explains the extraordinary wealth of wildlife flora and fauna it supports.

Cherry Cherry shop in Loddiswell

A Walk from Loddiswell

There are two possible places to begin this walk. The first (and longer) walk starts at Loddiswell Church, taking the old road which runs between Loddiswell and the river via Avon Mill—the second starting point for this glorious riverside woodland walk, which in spring is simply drenched with bluebells.

1. Loddiswell Church From the church, a lane runs down the back of the village. Traffic is scarce and the descent quite steep. The lane emerges at the Mill, the site of **Avon Mill Garden Centre**. It is possible to park a car here for a shorter woodland walk. This nursery has a wide selection of plants, trees and shrubs which are very well cared for. There is also the small but immensely popular **Coffee Shop**, which also serves fine light lunches. The taking of cake here is an essential part of the outing—but should it be taken before or after the walk? **Avon Mill, Woodleigh Road ☎ 01548 550338.**

2. From **Avon Mill** turn left on to the road. It is little more than a five minute walk to Loddiswell Station, which is now a private house, The gateway into the woods is to the right of the station—marked 'Woodland Walk' on the OS map. This woodland was the first to be purchased by the Woodland Trust. Established by a local man called Charles Watkins, a large new woodland has been planted nearby in his memory. The route follows the old Primrose Line railway track, which once ran (briefly) between South Brent, Loddiswell and Kingsbridge. The going is fairly easy, and the fast-flowing River Avon alongside offers plenty of dipping and 'pooh sticks' opportunities. In spring, the wood is carpeted with ramsoms (wild garlic). Take a deep breath, and imagine you're in a French kitchen. Although few people collect it, it has been seen for sale at a famous deli in Covent Garden priced at £3.50 for a small bunch. Gather the strong-smelling leaves and just

YELLOW OCHRE

Both the interior and exterior of many cottages in the area were painted in yellow ochre, which was dug from fields named East Ochre, West Ochre and South Ochre. It came in two colours: yellow from the clay, and red where the ochre had been tinted by iron deposits. It was processed by John and Henry Luscombe, 'Refiners of Colours', around the 1830s. Still in the paint business, H. Luscombe and Son, at 19 Fore Street, Kingsbridge, remains a family business 160 years on.

use as garlic, leeks or spring onion. Good in salads, in a cheese sandwich, or thrown in at the last minute in a creamy sauce to go with pasta.

The walk ends at Topsham Bridge, some two miles up the river. There's no option of a circular walk, so it's back the same way, but no less delightful in reverse.

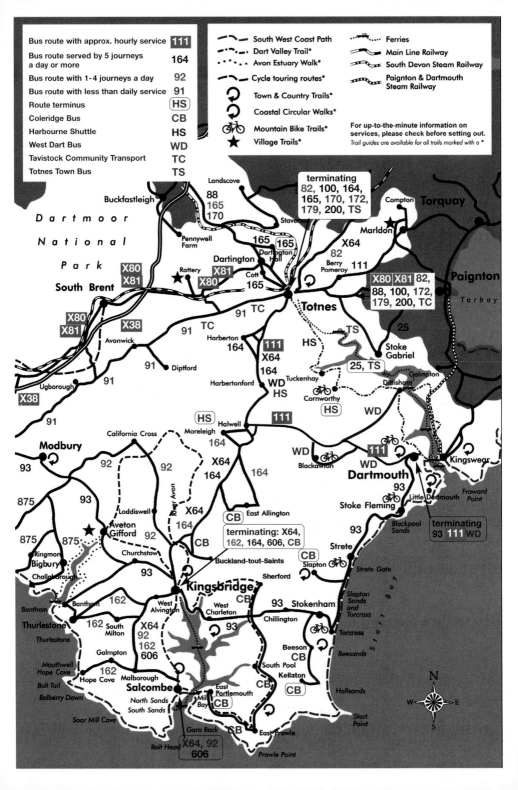

Appendices

Transport

If you travel to the South Hams by car, there's no need to spend hours of your holiday stuck behind the wheel. Often the best way to explore the area is by public transport. There are many modes of transport on offer: you can take a cruise up the estuaries, link a walk with a return bus or steam train trip and avoid the hassle of finding a parking place or driving in narrow lanes. The South Devon AONB Service's 'Out and About in The South Hams' leaflets make linking it all together easy. The free leaflet is available from many local cafés, pubs and information centres and gives more details on transport options than described here.

Buses
The map shows the main bus routes in the area, but note that times and fares—and sometimes routes—change frequently. For days out, it's best to concentrate on the routes which offer more than one journey per day, although with planning you can use less frequent services to advantage. . Best to pick up a South Hams area timetable from the local Tourist Information Centre or library. These give details of services offered by commercial companies and community buses.

When, where and how?
Most of the services in the area are operated by the First Group, but you will also find some routes served by Tally Ho! (around the Salcombe–Kingsbridge Estuary), Stagecoach Devon (Kingswear to Torbay), the Stoke Bus (Stoke Gabriel to Paignton only) and several community buses (see overleaf). For details of routes and timetables for the commercial operators call **Traveline ☎ 0870 608 2 608** (open from 7 am till 9 pm, 364 days a year). **www.traveline.org.uk.**

Cheaper Ways to Travel
There are lots of ways to cut the cost of travelling by bus:

• Day returns usually offer savings and can be bought on the bus.
• First Group offer 1 or 7 day 'Explorer' ticket for unlimited travel on First Services throughout South Devon and Cornwall.
• If you are a senior citizen or a person with disabilities, and you live in Devon, you should be eligible for a 'Devonwide' bus pass which entitles

you to half price fares throughout the county. Phone the Countywide Enquiry Line ☎ 01392 383688 (calls charged at local rate) for full details.

Community Buses
Several community-run buses provide services from the more outlying villages into towns. If you live in the following villages, phone for details:

- The Coleridge Bus (CB) links many villages on the east side of the Salcombe-Kingsbridge Estaury including Chillington, East Prawle, South Pool, Torcross, etc. ☎ 01548 853959
- The Harbourne Shuttle (HS) links Ashprington, Cornworthy, Harbertonford, Halwell and Morleigh to Totnes ☎ 01803 732092
- The West Dart Bus (WD) links Dittisham and Blackawton to Dartmouth, Totnes, Kingsbridge and Newton Abbot ☎ 01803 712424
- The Totnes Town Bus (TS) provides a service around the town 4 days a week and a llink to Stoke Gabriel on Fridays ☎ 01803 865211

Bus Company Contact Numbers
First Group ☎ 01752 402060 (open 7 days a week) • Tally Ho! ☎ 01548 853081 • Stagecoach Devon ☎ 01803 613226 • Stoke Bus ☎ 01803 554927.

Taxis
If you can't get a bus, consider taking a taxi. When there's a group of you, it can be cheaper than using a bus. Tourist Information Centres have lists of local taxi firms.

Walking and Cycling
There's a large range of walking guides produced by the South Devon AONB Service, covering from a short stroll to a week's hike. The prices range from 50p to £2.50—not bad for several days out! Call in at any Tourist Information Centre, which will have a good local selection, or phone Ivybridge Tourist Information Centre, who offer a mail order service: ☎ 01752 897035. There are cycle route guides too. The routes are on roads, but follow quiet lanes and byways, and a special pack details mountain bike routes for the more adventurous.

Cycle Hire
Cycle hire companies change fast. We therefore advise readers to contact their local Tourist Information Centre for a list of cycle hire companies.

Park and Ride
In Dartmouth and Salcombe there are Park and Ride schemes during the high season. They are well signposted as you enter the towns.

Crossing the Water
Because ferries are dependent on tides and weather, we advise that you check the times and availability of ferry services—see the table on pages 162–3.

Seasonal Calendar

Participate in local events! Seasonal celebrations and events are usually advertised in the local papers (see opposite).

Spring
Spring flower arrangements in churches at Eastertime • Jumble sales • Bluebell woods at Loddiswell • *Magnolia Campbellii* at Overbecks • Crocus circle under the turkey oak at Dartington Hall Gardens (February) • Camellia walks at Greenway gardens • Easter fairs • Spring plant sales • Art Week in Dartmouth • Dawn chorus walks (May) • Artists' open houses in Totnes and Harbertonford (May) • Craft fairs • Gardens open to the public • Friday afternoon walks at Coleton Fishacre.

Summer
Horticultural shows • Regattas and firework displays • Village fêtes • Music festivals at Salcombe, Kingsbridge and Malborough • Carnivals • Agricultural shows • Playgoers' Shakespeare Production in Dartington Hall gardens • Ways With Words Literary Festival at Dartington Hall • Dartington Summer School of Music.

Autumn
Harvest festivals and Harvest suppers • Village bonfire night celebrations • Apple Day celebrations or fairs (October 21st) • Riverford Farm's Pumpkin Day • Jumble sales • Dartmouth Food Festival.

Winter
Fatstock shows • Village pantomimes • Church concerts • Christmas fairs: Crux Craft Fair, Steiner School Christmas Market in Staverton, St Nicholas Fair in Kingsbridge • Wassailing at Stoke Gabriel.

Information

Local Papers
South Hams Newspapers publish the following local papers every Friday: *Kingsbridge and Salcombe Gazette, Totnes Times,* and *Dartmouth Chronicle.* South Hams Newspapers ☎ 01548 853101.

Tourist Information Centres (TICs)
Kingsbridge, The Quay ☎ 01548 853195.
Dartmouth: The Engine House, Mayors Avenue ☎ 01803 834224.
Totnes: The Town Mill ☎ 01803 863168.
Salcombe: Council Hall, Market Street ☎ 01548 843927.

Events

National Trust
Talks walks and performances are programmed at National Trust properties. Enquiries and information ☎ 01392 881691.

South Devon AONB Events
Paddle down the Avon by moonlight, construct a willow shelter, pick your own wild food supper, see a traditional wassail or listen to local stories. . . . the AONB Service produces an increasingly irresistible programme of events for all seasons. Pick up a programme at local village shops and Tourist Information Centres. For details ☎ 01803 861140.

English Heritage
The English Heritage diary of special events runs between April and the end of October, featuring activities, events and entertainments at sites in Dartmouth and Totnes. These include the hardy group of Living History players, who set up camp at Dartmouth Castle and live and eat 17th century-style, with occasional frenzied firing of muskets as re-enactments of civil war battles rage around the castle walls. For information on these and other events contact Dartmouth Castle ☎ 01803 833588 or Totnes Castle ☎ 01803 684406.

Slapton Ley Field Studies Centre

Regular walks and nature safaris are run during the summer months in and around the exceptional nature reserve at Slapton. Ideal for families. ☎ 01548 580466.

The Ramblers Association (see Kingsbridge outings)

They hold regular walks in and around the South Hams. For details contact the General Secretary, Mr L Baker ☎ 01548 580033, or contact the local TIC for details.

Gardens Open to the Public

Each year the National Gardens Scheme publish a 'yellow book', which details dates and times of Devon gardens open to the public. Available in bookshops and TICs.

Pantomimes

Cheer up those post-Christmas blues: the end of January into February is the local panto season. Talents of all kinds and of all ages are pooled in these small scale productions, and what might be lacking in performance skills is made up for in sheer effort, energy and enthusiasm. Those months of evening and weekend rehearsals pay off in performances when the audience—made up largely of family and friends—throw themselves into the booing the baddie and 'behind you' routines. Watch out for Malborough, Blackawton, Cornworthy, Dittisham and Harberton.

From the Farm Gate

Buying vegetables and meat direct from producers has become part of the weekly routine for many in the South Hams. There are a number of different options available. Here are just some of them:

Vegetable Boxes

Old Cuming Farm A small scale operation. These boxes of excellent quality organic produce are hand-packed to the customer's budget and requirements. For visitors to the South Hams, boxes may be ordered by telephone, and picked up from the farm. **Old Cuming Farm, Colston Road, Buckfastleigh** ☎ 01364 642672.

Riverford Farm One of the first organic vegetable box schemes to have been established in the UK, Riverford boxes come in three sizes. Added to the weekly staples of carrots, potatoes and onions, are a range of seasonal salads and vegetables. It's done on a 'get what you're given' basis, and the quality of produce is unfailingly high. **Riverford Farm Organic Vegetables, Wash Barn, Buckfastleigh ☎ 01803 762720.**

Meat and Poultry Direct
Phil Bond, Collaton Down, Blackawton ☎ **01803 712636.**
Jill Rowden, Lower Norton Farm, Blackawton ☎ **01803 835458.**
Lower Washbourne Geese ☎ **01803 732765.**
Malcolm Patey, Westleigh Barton, Harberton ☎ **01803 863442.**

Farmers Markets
A good source of all kinds of local produce.
- Totnes Farmers Market, Totnes Civic Hall, last Saturday in the month.
- Kingsbridge Farmers Market, The Quay, first Saturday in the month. Contact Carol Trant ☎ **01803 861202.**
- Buckfastleigh Farmers Market, every Thursday. Contact Richard Rogers ☎ **01803 762674.**

Booklist

The Birds and Natural History of the South Hams by Gordon Waterhouse, Orchard Books, 2000.
The Book of Loddiswell: a photographic history of the Parish, Halsgrove Press, 1999.
Dartmouth and its Neighbours by Ray Freeman, Phillimore, 1990.
Dartmouth—a Brief Historical Guide by Tom Jaine, Dartmouth & Kingswear Society, 1996.
Dittisham Village Guide, Dittisham Parish Council, revised 1996.
Devon Building by Peter Beacham, Devon Books, 1990.
Discovering Green Lanes by Valerie Belsey, Green Books 2001.
The Elmhirsts of Dartington by Michael Young, Routledge & Kegan Paul, 1982, reprinted by Dartington Hall Trust, 1996.
Exploring Green Lanes in the South Hams by Valerie Belsey, Green Books 2003.

A Fortunate Place: A History of Slapton by Robin Stanes, Field Studies Council, 1983.
The Good Town of Totnes by Percy Russell, Devonshire Association, 1963.
Hallsands: a Pictorial History by Sugden Designs, 1984.
History of Kingsbridge and Salcombe by Ann Born, Phillimore, 1986. (Currently out of print, but worth asking for in second hand bookshops)
Kingsbridge, Devon by Ann Born & Kathy Tanner, 1986.
Kingsbridge and surroundings, Sarah Prideaux Fox, 1874.
Kingsbridge Estuary with rambles in the neighbourhood, Sarah Prideaux Fox, 1864, reprinted by Cookworthy Museum 1982.
Magic Tree: Devon Garden Plants—History and Conservation, Devon Books/NCCPG 1989.
Salcombe and Neighbourhood by James Fairweather, third edition, 1912.
Secret Nature of Devon by Andrew Cooper, Green Books, 2005.
Story of Thurlestone, Bantham & West Buckland by Kendal McDonald, 1993.
The Tragedy of Hallsands Village by John L Harvey.
Wildlife of the Dart Estuary by Tony Soper, Harbour Books, 1982.
Wildlife of the Kingsbridge & Salcombe Estuary by Gordon Waterhouse Orchard Books, 1999.
Wildlife Walks In the South Hams by Gordon Waterhouse, Orchard Books, 2002.

FERRY TIMETABLES

Please note these are subject to change. At River Avon Passenger Ferry, look for information boards by ferry slips.

Type of Ferry	Operating Period	Operating times	Routes	Contact
RIVER AVON				
River Avon passenger ferry (see note above)	Easter to September	Mon–Sat am & pm. No Sunday service. Check times.	Bantham slipway to Cockleridge Ham (Bigbury-on-Sea)	Neil Schroeter 01548 561196 Mon–Fri 9 am–4.30 pm
SALCOMBE–KINGSBRIDGE ESTUARY				
Salcombe–East Portlemouth passenger ferry	all year	daily between 8 am–5.30 pm	Salcombe Pier (ferry steps) to East Portlemouth jetty	Ray Shortman 01548 842061
RIVER DART (1)				
Kingsbridge–Salcombe Estuary cruiser/ passenger ferry	May–September	scheduled timetable (times vary according to tides—details from Tourist Info Centres	Kingsbridge town quay or Kingsbridge boatyard quay to Salcombe pier	Peter Moule (Rivermaid) 01548 853525/ 853607
Salcombe–South Sands passenger ferry	Easter–October	daily: half hourly service between 9.45 am and 5.15 pm	Salcombe pier (ferry steps), Salcombe Whitestrand, to South Sands beach	Tim Tucker 01548 561035
Lower Dartmouth vehicle ferry	daily all year	continuous service 7 am–10.45 pm (8 am–10.55 pm Sundays)	Kingswear to Dartmouth South Embankment	South Hams District Council 01803 752342
Higher Dartmouth vehicle ferry	daily all year	continuous service 6.30 am–10.45 pm (8 am–11.45 pm Sundays)	Dartmouth North Embankment to Kingswear Britannia Halt	Kerry Southern Philip 01803 833351

FERRY TIMETABLES

Type of Ferry	Operating Period	Operating times	Routes	Contact
RIVER DART (2)				
Dartmouth Castle passenger ferry	Easter–end October	daily 10 am –5 pm on demand—every few minutes when busy	Dartmouth South embankment to Dartmouth Castle	Julian Distin 01803 835034
Dartmouth– Dittisham– Greenway passenger ferry	Over Easter, then Whitsun to end September	daily service— approx hourly from 10 am to 4.30 pm (phone for times)	Dartmouth North Embankment to Dittisham pontoon & Greenway	Dart Pleasure Craft (David Ridalls) 0781 8001108
Dartmouth– Greenway– Stoke Gabriel– Sharpham vineyard	Mid May to October	scheduled trips programme available from Dartmouth Tourist Info Centre	Dartmouth embankment upriver	River Explorer 07768 846605
Dittisham– Greenway passenger ferry	all year	daily: 7.30 am –9 pm summer (7.30 am–5 pm winter)—ring bell at Dittisham or phone to book in advance	Dittisham & Greenway Quay	Greenway Ferry Service 01803 844010
Totnes– Dartmouth passenger cruisers	April–October	scheduled timetables (times vary with tides)— information on quaysides and Tourist Info Centres	between Totnes Steamer Quay & Dartmouth South embankment	Riverlink 01803 834488
Kingswear– Dartmouth passenger ferry	all year	daily regular service 7 am–11 pm (9 am–11 pm Sundays)	Dartmouth (by Station Restaurant) to Kingswear (by railway station	Riverlink 01803 834488

Index

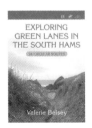